Dead Centre: How political pragmatism is killing us

First published in 2025 by Australia Institute Press
Reprinted 2026

ISBN 978-1-7636621-4-8 (print)
ISBN 978-1-7636621-5-5 (ebook)

Published in Australia and New Zealand by
Australia Institute Press
www.australiainstitute.org.au

Cataloguing-in-publication data is available from the National Library of Australia

Proofread by Rod Morrison

Printed and bound in Australia by McPherson's Printing Group, an accredited ISO AS/NZS 14001 Environmental Management Systems printer.

Dead Centre: How political pragmatism is killing us

Richard Denniss

Australia Institute Press

Democracy thrives on high expectations and starves on a diet of cynicism. But for decades the lowest common denominator of "centrism" has stifled serious debate about what kind of country we want to be and how best to get there. We are one of the richest countries in the world, yet our health, education and public transport systems are a pale imitation of what many Europeans enjoy. We are the second largest energy exporter in the world, but while the Saudis, Qataris and Norwegians get rich when world energy prices surge, we watch our power and petrol bills soar and our elected leaders pretend there is nothing they can do to help. We are the twelfth largest economy in the world and claim to be punching above our weight on the world stage when in reality we are barely raising a glove. Maybe Australians are happy with the way things are, but I suspect not.

The endless centrist droning about the need for tax reform and a productivity agenda stifles genuine debate about what Australians want more of, what we want less of, and how to redesign our system of taxes, subsidies and publicly provided services in ways that would deliver happier, healthier and richer lives for the vast majority of us. Rather than actively participate in democratic debates about whether we should have a health system that is more like that of the US or Norway, most Australians have been bored into silence by the endless technocratic econobabble about fiscal sustainability and effective marginal tax rates when the truth is Australia can easily afford to have the nice things they have in Europe.

Labor's recent landslide victory in the lower house, combined with the majority it can form with the ten Greens senators whenever they agree in the upper house, means there is simply no progressive reform the prime minister can get through his own party room that the Coalition can veto. The 2025 election result provides the Albanese Government with the opportunity to be either the most progressive parliament in modern history, the dampest of squibs, or the centre of the centrists. The choice is Labor's.

John Howard never gave Labor a veto of his reforms and in turn he did whatever he needed, including radically amending his GST plan to get it through the Senate. He bribed Senator Mal Colston to quit the Labor Party and sit as an independent. The price was providing Liberal support for Colston's nomination for the well-paid position of Deputy President of the Senate, and the legislative dividend for Howard was Colston's vote to privatise Telstra.

Likewise, when Anthony Albanese was serious about reform, as he was with industrial relations in his first term, he was happy to cut a deal with the Greens. Indeed, the idea that Labor would have waited for bipartisan support from the Liberals before delivering the "Secure Jobs, Better Pay" or "Closing Loopholes" bills is simply absurd. But when it came to environmental policy, climate policy, electoral reform and the powers of the promised corruption watchdog Labor was happy to let the Liberals veto Labor's ambitions. In those instances, it was Labor's preference for dealing with the Liberals that led to watered-down legislation.

No major party MP gets preselected, elected, promoted to cabinet or installed in the top job without knowing how to count votes in their branch, their electorate and their party room.

Knowing the voting rules and knowing how to count the votes *is* the job. And every prime minister knows that an ugly win is still a win. The single vote that made Tony Abbott opposition leader in 2009 did nothing to diminish the impact he went on to have.

And all prime ministers know how to look like they are trying. Like a call-centre worker claiming that your call is important to them, all professional politicians can say they are hard at work on their publicly stated priorities while doing nothing to actually deliver on them. Most people understand that bold speeches, summits and inquiries can conceal a lack of ambition behind a cloak of activity. But few people realise that introducing legislation to parliament, legislation designed in such a way that it will not pass through the Senate, is the secret weapon of Australian politics. Used well, such strategically drafted legislation, sometimes called "bluff bills", can convince the whole country that a government is desperate to do something that it would rather leave undone.

The best bluff bills are designed to make the government seem centrist and paint their opponents as extreme. It is easy for outsiders to confuse the willingness of a government to introduce legislation to parliament with their determination to fight for an actual outcome. The key skill of university debaters is to sound like they care about the case they are making, and our parliament is full of former university debaters.

No one negotiating a free trade agreement, an enterprise agreement, or even the purchase of a second-hand car expects their first offer to be accepted. Likewise, any government that drops a piece of legislation into parliament and says "respect my mandate" isn't serious about driving change. Like gorillas thumping their chests in lieu of a real fight, governments often thump their tables and shout "mandate" in lieu of engaging with the Senate as our Constitution demands.

Labor has become particularly skilled at playing "the game of per cents", drafting legislation that focuses debate on arbitrary percentage targets (or sometimes amounts of expenditure) which are designed at the outset to draw criticism from the Greens on the basis that Labor is not doing enough and from the Coalition arguing Labor is going too far. Having used their arbitrary targets to extract the desired response from their parliamentary opponents, Labor is then free to claim that, like Goldilocks sampling porridge in the three bears' house, their arbitrary policy settings must be just right in the sensible centre. Such a strategy delivers good optics, but it delivers little reform.

While the media tends to applaud any advocate arguing they are in the sensible centre, perhaps because the business model of much of the legacy media was to be inoffensive to a broad audience to maximise advertising revenue, what rarely attracts attention in the acres of Australian political analysis is how arbitrary the definition of centrism is. Indeed, the concepts of left and right are fundamentally inadequate when addressing the biggest issues facing modern democracies. Why, for example, are right-wing European parties more ambitious than the ALP on climate? And since when did freedom of speech and transparency around government spending become left-wing issues?

The media's silence on the contradiction between the pursuit of centrism and the pursuit of evidence-based policy is even more jarring. For example:

- If evidence overwhelmingly suggests mandatory sentencing of children is a bad idea, then is it centrist for Labor to ignore that evidence and support mandatory detention of children on the basis that the Greens are opposed to it and the Coalition want even tougher mandatory sentences than Labor?
- If the scientific evidence says building new gas and coal projects is harmful for the climate then is it centrist for Labor to ignore that evidence and support new gas and coal projects because the Greens are opposed to them and the Coalition promise to approve them even faster?
- If evidence shows increases in domestic violence and inequality result from problem gambling, then is it centrist to put off changing legislation around gambling advertising because there is a forthcoming election?

While it is rarely discussed, the legacy media's interest in evidence-based policy only exists in a narrow range of circumstances, primarily situations in which powerful groups are pushing the evidence. For example, when the Business Council of Australia use modelling to show tax cuts for their members would deliver economic benefits in the future, policymakers take them far more seriously than when public health professionals provide evidence that greater investment in preventative health will deliver long-run benefits to the same economy. Economic modelling, and the way the media covers it, is a great way to make political power more palatable by dressing up self-interest as national interest.

Regardless of the views of the current generation of politicians, or of the views of those in other powerful positions that the legacy media defers to, scientific evidence simply doesn't respect the arbitrary positions that political parties temporarily adopt. Labor understands this, which is why they acted on the science (and the urging of the CFMEU) to ban artificial stone benchtops based on the risk to worker health. In that instance Labor didn't set a benchtop reduction target or develop a benchtop transition plan. Perhaps most significantly, Labor did not depict calls for a ban, based on science and disruptive to those who profit from selling benchtops, as extreme. Labor also demonstrated its willingness and ability to act decisively — and in the face of industry opposition — in their support for a social-media ban for kids under 16 during the last parliament. Likewise, in the past Labor has supported bans on asbestos and whaling. Would a party that celebrates centrism make the same decisions today?

Commentators often ask about "evidence" for policy decisions without reflecting on the fact that evidence clearly matters more in some cases (benchtops) than in others (mandatory sentencing of children). Why is it that evidence matters in some cases but not others? The most obvious answer, that evidence only matters when groups with political power aren't threatened by it, is too cynical for most centrists to abide. Without that answer, how else could you explain gas and coal expansion, gas and coal subsidies or the hesitancy to implement a ban on gambling advertising? How do centrists explain why no amount of scientific evidence or public support for such changes has ever led the legacy media to call the legacy political parties extreme in their determination to resist popular, evidence-based change?

Given the faith that centrists themselves like to place in evidence-based policy perhaps it is just too painful for them to admit that those with real power get to decide when our policy processes pretend to care about evidence, and when we are forced to ignore it. The ultimate irony for proponents of evidence-based policy is that there is no evidence in Australia that evidence ever defeats political power when it is time for hard choices to be made. And the ultimate manifestation of political power in Australia is the ability to get both major parties to agree that some questions, and some answers, are simply too extreme to be taken seriously, even in the face of scientific consensus. While it may be comforting to believe that if only a minister understood the evidence of harm from gambling, gas expansion or locking up children that policy change would be inevitable; such magical thinking distracts those who are serious about driving change from the hard democratic work of putting even more pressure on ministers than politically successful industries do.

The big bluff

We are all shaped by our experiences. As a rule, I don't rely on private conversations to support my public conclusions, but in this instance, I think it will be helpful to recount one anonymised conversation I had with a Howard Government minister back when I was Chief of Staff to the then leader of the Australian Democrats, Senator Natasha Stott Despoja.

At the time the Democrats held nine Senate seats and the balance of power in the Senate, meaning that if the Howard Government wanted to make a new law and Labor was opposed to that law then it was the Democrats who decided whether, and in what amended form, such a law would pass the Senate.

One night I met with a senior Howard minister to discuss a piece of forthcoming legislation. A "draft bill", as they are known, had yet to be circulated but the government had signalled its legislative intentions and it was, for the government, safe to assume the Democrats would, like Labor, oppose the proposed legislation.

Which is precisely what made the late-night meeting interesting.

After dispensing with the usual pleasantries of gossiping about other parties and probing for intel about unrelated matters we got down to business. The cabinet minister handed me a draft bill on letterhead and said, "You guys are going to hate this bill. We obviously want you to vote for it as is … but I reckon a clever man like you would be able to come up with a range of amendments that my party could live with."

The minister then handed me second pile of papers, printed on plain paper with no coat of arms at the top, which listed a raft of amendments designed by the minister to significantly water down his own legislation.

We shared a laugh about the likely reaction from some of the members of his own party if they had been in the room with us that night. I suggested that while the amendments he proposed were a step in the right direction, I couldn't be sure that the Democrats would support the bill, even in amended form, and that

I would likely come up with some more ambitious amendments myself.

Formalities finished for the night, the minister performatively reiterated that his party was determined to see the bill pass in its original form and assured me that the Coalition would fight hard against any amendments. I told him I looked forward to the lengthy battle to improve his bill. The meeting concluded with our shared assessment that the ideological obsessions of some in his party had a galvanising benefit for both the Democrats and the Coalition.

The minister's original bluff bill, a proposal he knew would never pass the Senate, gave both parties something to keep their party rooms, and their voters, focused on and agitated by. The careful drafting of a piece of legislation designed from the outset to never pass the parliament would provide months of good media coverage for both the Liberals and the Democrats, coverage which would send a clear message to both parties' potential voters about how hard each party was fighting for its principles. Unsurprisingly, the bill never passed.

Politics is not what it looks like on the news.

Prime ministers know much better than you

or I how many options they have to create the appearance of activity and determination necessary to manipulate their backbench, stakeholders and voters alike into thinking they are fighting the good fight while promising powerful groups that they have no need to fear any change.

A bad map can be worse than no map

"A bad map is worse than no map at all for it engendered in the traveler a false confidence and might easily cause him to set aside these instincts which would otherwise guide him if he would but place himself in their care."
Cormac McCarthy — The Crossing

Like an old street directory, the left/right/centre map of Australian politics is dated, disorienting and dangerously incomplete. Just as suburbs now sit where farms were just 30 years ago, the traditional map of Australian politics is more likely to cause confusion than clarity, especially for the 12.5 million people who have moved to Australia or turned 18 since John Howard beat Paul Keating in 1996. Our country, and the issues it faces, have changed radically since then, but the map those who analyse our politics most commonly use still harks back to a Hawke-Keating era that few voting Australians experienced and even fewer care about.

The search for the sensible centre of Australian politics is as proud and pointless as the colonial search for the great inland sea: smart people claiming a noble cause pressing on while ignoring all the evidence around them and distracting Australians from the real options staring them in the face.

The belief that there are clear lines between left- and right-wing people and issues is built into the way most commentators describe Australia's democracy. We talk about a pendulum swinging between left and right. We make one third of the votes cast disappear by converting them into an artificial two-party preferred vote. And the ABC insists on presenting just two sides of arguments even when there are three or four. Indeed, when it comes to climate science the ABC insists on presenting two sides when there is only one.

Of course, there are times when the idea of left and right provides a powerful, if limited, lens through which to understand Australian policy and political debates. But the idea that it is left wing to oppose public funding of nuclear power and right wing to provide free gas to foreign gas companies has no basis in philosophy, history, economics or anything else.

Unsurprisingly, the left/right/centre framework is at its most useful when examining issues that led to the formation of Australia's political parties in the first place; worker rights, the taxation of capital and the provision of services to citizens all lend themselves to analysis along a left/right spectrum. While the term "left wing" originally described those Republican members of the French National Assembly who sat on the left of the chamber, while supporters of the monarchy sat on the right, in Australia the term has generally been applied to parties supporting the rights of workers to strike for better pay, greater reliance on the collection of taxes on capital, and greater public expenditure on essential services. "Centrism" is the idea that neither left nor right ideologies are correct and that aiming for a middle road is the best option. But as this essay shows, there simply is no centrist option in many of the most critical debates in contemporary Australian politics. Likewise, this essay argues that the search for centrist compromise can be weaponised by those hoping to keep things just as they are.

Historically, the binary of the left/right spectrum played an important part in Australian politics. In 1891 the Labor Electoral League in New South Wales became the first Labor party elected to a parliament in the world. In response, Menzies formed the Liberal Party out of grab-bag group of non-Labor parties containing adherents of protectionism, free trade and the prevailing Keynesian way of thinking. The Liberal Party really was a broad church back then.

As a result of that history there have been two sides in Australian parliaments for a long time. But Australia's long tradition of having two major parties, defined largely in opposition to each other, does not mean there is an inherent logic behind which party happens to support an individual's right to have an abortion, marry the adult of their choosing, or the right to have access to fresh air or clean water.[1] The consequence of this is that if there is no clear division of contemporary issues on the left/right spectrum then there simply is no meaningful centre.

Bad maps don't just disorient, they define the territory in ways that conceal rather than reveal. They keep us looking down at old debates rather than looking up to observe what is really going on around us. By obsessing over centrism and using an outdated map, we stifle discussion of many of the biggest questions our democracy needs to address, and we ignore a wide range of possible solutions.

Australia is one of the richest countries in the world and, even after adjusting for inflation, our annual GDP has grown by 253 per cent since Bob Hawke was elected in 1983. Yet we regularly hear that we still can't afford to have the nice things we once took for granted. In the 1930s, in the midst of the Depression, Australian governments were building beautiful ocean baths that we swim in today, for free! But somehow the sensible centre has convinced us that the only way we can afford a nice pool today is for governments to go into a public–private consortium with an investment bank and a superannuation fund and, obviously, charge a fee to swim in it so that the super fund can generate 10 per cent returns forever more. Neoliberalism's best trick was to make the residents of a rich country feel poor.

Why don't we feel rich when the world price of our energy exports soar?

Why do we have to be one of the lowest tax countries in the developed world?

To ask such questions is to place yourself outside of the sensible centre of Australian public debate. But anyone with access to the internet can see that other sensible countries have made radically different decisions from our own, and as a result, other countries have radically different societies to ours, often with free childcare, no private school fees and no private health insurance.

Imagine if we didn't give more than half the gas we export away for free and chose to provide free childcare and free healthcare as a solution to a "cost of living crisis". While other countries do exactly that, in Australia it is impolite, simplistic or even naïve to point out that Norway heavily taxes their fossil fuel industry and gives their kids free higher education while in Australia we subsidise our fossil fuel industry and charge our kids a fortune to go to university. Some have argued that it is easy for Norway to tax their fossil fuel industry because there is bipartisan support for doing so!

Fitting in

Just because everyone is doing something doesn't make it right. If Australia had a whaling industry and there was bipartisan support for it as a job creator, would it be centrist to support whaling? Does bipartisan political support for whaling in Japan make it a good idea? What would an Australian centrist who moved to Japan think is right?

When I was a kid, I often tried to excuse my poor decision-making by pointing out that I'd simply done what all my friends were doing. My mum's standard response was to ask me if I would stick my head in an oven if all my friends were doing that too. That's why I've never been a centrist; my mum, a lifelong Liberal voter, taught me not just to think for myself, but that it was dangerous to simply follow the thinking of others, including (to her endless political frustration) her own.

For many Australians, fitting in with those currently in power is far more important than frank and fearless advice. The price many in Australia are willing to pay to gain access to those we have placed in charge is the promise *not* to speak truth to power. A prime minister grants privileges by giving a one-on-one media interview, appointing someone chief scientist or departmental secretary. But those privileges aren't handed out randomly, or lightly, and they invariably go to those with a safe pair of centrist hands. No journalist with close access to Anthony Albanese has asked if he regrets founding, or leaving, the Parliamentary Friends of Palestine. It would be impolite to call Anthony Albanese a climate-change sceptic or a science denier. He knows that, and so does every journalist in Australia. But what no one knows is what to call a prime minister who supports politically easy climate policies (such as renewable energy subsidies) but ignores hard ones (such as stopping the construction of brand-new gas and coal mines in areas that have never produced gas or coal). In Australia we tend to call someone like Anthony Albanese, who chooses to rely on climate science sometimes but ignores it at others, a centrist. It's a lot more polite.

Likewise, when one former chief scientist was questioned about what advice he gave the government about the dangers of opening new gas and coal mines to power Australian industry, he simply replied, "I was never asked".[2]

Centrism means fitting in. And fitting in means never making those in power look silly. Who cares that AUKUS became policy without parliamentary approval? It's done now, and centrists can't stand their ground once the centre shifts because their ground is defined by the decisions of others. The centre of politics can no more be found on a map than the centre of music can be found by flicking between radio stations.

The desperation of so many people to fit in with whatever is deemed centrist today would be sad if the consequences weren't so serious. When those with the ability, arguably the responsibility, to speak truth to power remain strategically silent, bad things happen. Bad actors find refuge. Bad policies become law. And bad deeds go unpunished. The costs are not just counted in the tens of billions of dollars, but by the loss of faith in our institutions, and indeed in democracy itself. In the most egregious cases, such as Robodebt, the costs are counted in human lives lost. We must remember that the first person charged for the war crimes committed by Australian soldiers is the whistleblower who alerted us to them.

Meaningless middle

Centrism sounds a lot nicer than extremism but to me supporting Nelson Mandela sounds a lot nicer than supporting apartheid. And supporting a science-based approach to climate change sounds a lot more sensible to me than supporting fossil fuel expansion because, like whaling and asbestos mining, there's some jobs in it. But to each their own. There is nothing in the Constitution that says we need to base our laws on being nice or listening to science.

Centrism isn't a philosophy, ideology or even a coherent approach to policy development. It is simply the willingness to let others define the breadth of what is politically acceptable and to choose from a policy menu written by those in power. Centrism makes democratic sense when trying to balance some irreconcilable conflicting desires; for example, some people want to ban loud motorbikes completely and some want to make their motorbikes even louder, so our elected representatives tend towards an arbitrary noise limit (centrism) rather than adopt an (extreme) ban or allow total freedom for individuals to make as much noise pollution as they want. Even though there is no right decibel limit for motorbikes, we can have a sensible debate about compromising on such things.

Should workers have unlimited rights to strike whenever they want over whatever they want? Or should strikes be illegal? Or should a democracy develop a centrist position on when it's okay to strike and when it's not? Most democratic countries have opted for somewhere in the middle, but few Australians likely realise that our laws make strike action far harder than in any other democratic country.[3] Would a change in our right to strike laws that took us closer to OECD norms be centrist or extremist?

But while the centrist instinct to compromise makes some sense for some issues, it is meaningless for many of the big questions democracies face.

What is the centrist position on slavery? Or abortion? How many jobs would whaling need to create before it became centrist again? Or slavery?

If centrism is your goal, then the key questions should surely be:

- Who defines the boundaries of where sensible options end and extreme ones begin? And;
- What is a centrist to do when those with power adopt more extreme positions? If power shifts its position do centrists have to follow?

Indeed, if parties such as Labor and organisations such as the ABC set centrism as their target, wouldn't that encourage parties such as the Greens, One Nation or even the Liberal Party to adopt more extreme positions in order to drag the sensible centre their way? Doesn't centrism reward extremism? Looking at the past 15 years, it seems that is exactly what the Coalition was doing as they steadily hardened their opposition to science-based climate policy, even as the scientific conclusions, and public support, strengthened.

No more safe seats

The pursuit of centrism has clearly left a lot of voters feeling poorly represented by the two major parties whose combined primary vote has trended steadily downwards for decades. Indeed, as discussed below, in 2025 Labor's record number of seats in the lower house came off the back of its second lowest primary vote since World War II.

Back in 2022 few thought it possible, especially those in the press gallery and the Liberal Party, for first-time independent candidates to win the safest Liberal seats in the country. But having lost six of their so-called "blue ribbon" seats to independents, including Mackellar which was held by Jason Falinski with a margin of 13.2 per cent on the old electoral pendulum, the common-sense view shifted quite quickly.

Falinski clearly learnt from his experience. Despite his large electoral margin, the former

Liberal frontbencher and former president of the NSW Liberal Party who lost to Dr Sophie Scamps, now believes the Liberal Party does not need to "focus on left or right", because most Australians do not "think along that sort of ideological spectrum".[4]

Similarly, in his post-election speech to the National Press Club, ALP National Secretary Paul Erickson highlighted how close independents came to winning the once-safe Labor seats of Bean in the ACT and Fremantle in Western Australia, even though there was a nationwide swing to Labor. These seats demonstrate how the political terrain in Australia is changing with Erickson agreeing that there is now no such thing as a safe seat.

The 2025 election not only reinforced the new reality that no seats are safe against the right candidate challenging an incumbent on the right issues, it also showed that the metaphorical pendulum, just like the grandfather clocks that once relied on them, is now out of date and little more than an historical curiosity. For decades the idea that there was a pendulum that represented the national mood which in turn gently knocked over marginal seats but rarely swung far enough to threaten safe seats has defined most pre-election and election night analysis. But as anyone who has watched Antony Green struggle to comprehend, let alone explain to viewers, what was happening in so-called "three-cornered contests" would know, Australian elections just aren't tidy anymore. If there ever was a pendulum, it is now better thought of as a wrecking ball, swinging in three dimensions rather than two and by turns knocking over safe and marginal seats, threatening all parties from all directions all at once.

The sustained surge in support for independents and minor parties over the past 40 years, and the steady decline in the primary vote of the major parties during the same period, reinforce the usefulness of the wrecking ball metaphor. Once upon a time the major parties typically won so-called "marginal seats" off each other, and almost never won or lost safe seats. But in recent times independent MPs have been more likely to win so-called safe seats than to win the classic marginals that the major parties fought endlessly over. One reason why the community independents have been so disruptive to politics as usual is the *type* of seats they have won, not just the number.

Once upon a time frontbench MPs in so-called safe seats had little to fear during elections. Just as generals rarely die in wars, up-and-coming leaders rarely lost their seats in parliament. But, as Tony Abbott, Josh Frydenberg and Jason Falinski found out, that's just not the case anymore. Since 2001, 82 per cent of all the seats that have changed hands and been won by major party candidates were seats defined by the Australian Electoral Commission (AEC) as marginal. By contrast, 79 per cent of the seats taken by minor party or independent candidates were defined by the AEC as safe or fairly safe seats.

While Labor won (or the Liberals lost) a record haul of seats in 2025, a closer look at the results shows how vulnerable, from multiple directions, many Labor seats now are. For example, Labor nearly lost some of its safest seats, such as Fremantle in Western Australia and the ACT seat of Bean to independents. And while they won Melbourne, Brisbane and Griffith from the Greens, they nearly lost Wills to the Greens who had swings to them in Wills, Richmond and a range of other lower house seats. Likewise, Labor beat the Liberals to win Bullwinkel in Western Australia with a margin of just 0.51 per cent. So should Labor defend itself against the Greens, independents or Liberals at the next election? While the old pendulum provided certainty, modern politics means Labor cannot simply shift to the left or right, and as the results in Bean and Fremantle make clear, they cannot afford to ignore the views of voters in what were once called safe seats. The last two elections have shown that no seat is safe from the right candidate running on the right issues.

The Liberals narrowly won the seat of Goldstein by 0.08 per cent, or around 175 votes, and lost the seat of Bradfield by 26 votes, both against independents focused on climate action. They lost to Labor in Bullwinkel by just 1,000. So, should they attack them for going too far on climate in order to win back "outer suburban seats" or should the Liberals attack Labor for approving too many fossil fuel projects in an attempt to win back Bradfield and hold Goldstein? Tim Wilson is going to have to make some hard choices about whether to listen to his voters or his friends in the fossil fuel industry if he wants to keep one of the most marginal seats in the country, but many of his National Party colleagues fear losing their seats to

Pauline Hanson's One Nation if they don't loudly proclaim their climate scepticism.

According to newly installed Liberal Leader Sussan Ley, "We will have a red-hot go at every seat that we don't hold at the next election — the teals, Labor marginals, inner suburban, outer suburban." While such a shotgun approach would seem to need some refinement, she is certainly right to avoid any strategy based on the smooth sweep of an imagined pendulum to identify her party's target seats.

The electoral pendulum is now of virtually no analytical use for understanding political strategy. At the end of this term of parliament, if a few thousand voters in a few dozen seats shift their votes then both the Labor and Liberal parties could lose seemingly safe seats to independents, minor parties or to each other. Indeed, now that the Liberal Party primary vote is at a record low of 28 per cent (including the LNP in Queensland and the CLP in the Northern Territory) and Labor's 2025 primary of 34.6 per cent only narrowly surpassed their 2022 nadir of 32.6 per cent, even small shifts in which candidates come second, third or even fourth in 2028 will have big impacts on who goes on to win seats in safe and marginal electorates alike. To be fair, it's not just rusted on election-watchers who find the role of third and fourth placed candidates confusing, but regardless of how confusing the commentariat find close contests between multiple candidates, the AEC knows how to count them, even if it takes more than three weeks in close races like Calwell, Bradfield and Goldstein. Close counts taking weeks to finalise might ruin the theatre for celebrity psephologists on election night, but they are the clearest proof that no matter where we live, all our votes are important, and thanks to preferential voting, no votes can ever be wasted.

But while few understand how the electoral pendulum is calculated, and even fewer understand its implications, the media's preferred electoral indicator — the "two-party preferred vote", or 2PP — conceals the most significant trends occurring in Australian politics. By design, the two-party preferred indicator treats all votes for minor parties and independents as if they were simply truck stops on the way to the final destination of electing a major party MP. And of course, bad maps lead to bad navigation.

It is true that when the record number of

votes for the Greens, other minor parties and independents are allocated to the two major parties (even in seats the major parties lost) to create the 2PP, the Labor Party 2PP is among its highest ever. But in reality, while Bob Hawke's Labor attracted 49.5 per cent of the first preference votes cast in 1983, and Kevin Rudd won 43.4 per cent in 2007, Anthony Albanese's triumphant victory was based on a nationwide primary vote of just 34.6 per cent. Indeed, Albanese's record share of lower house seats distracts from the fact that the primary vote swing to Labor is less than half that achieved under Bill Hayden (1980), Bob Hawke (1983), Paul Keating (1993) or Kevin Rudd (2007).

There has been a steady decline in Labor's primary vote, compensated for by an increased reliance on the preferences of those voters who, by definition, would prefer to have a minor party or independent MP represent them but will settle for Labor over the Coalition. As shown in the figure below, in 2025 Anthony Albanese won a record high percentage of lower house seats off a near record low primary vote.

Put simply, in 2019 Bill Shorten won a larger percentage of the primary vote than Albanese,

Labor's first-preference vote compared to Labor's share of the seats in the House of Representatives, 1983 to 2025

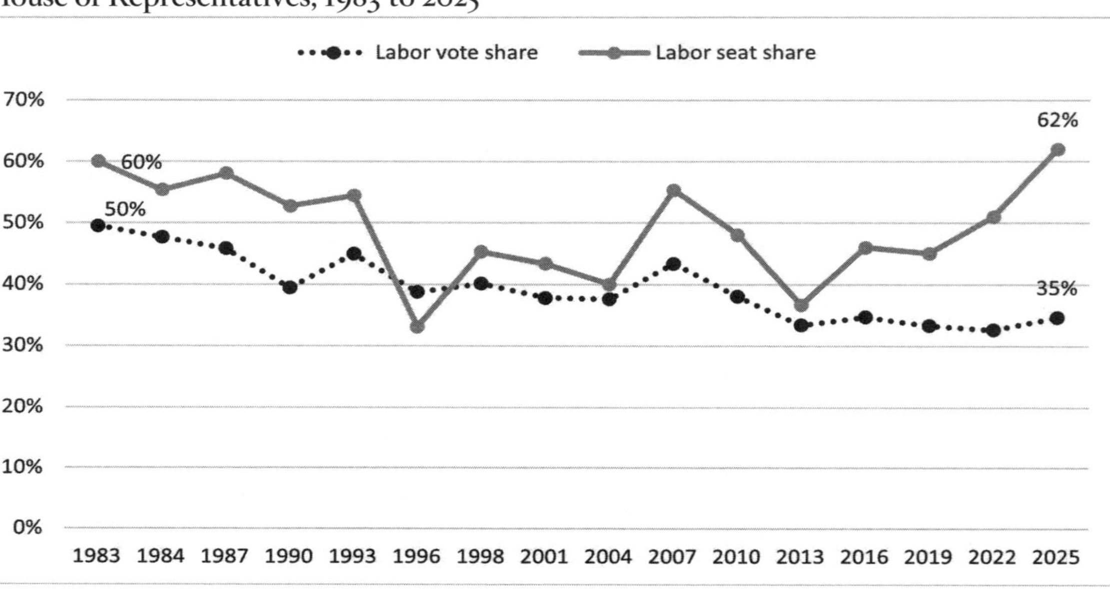

but Albanese won more seats than any Labor leader since Curtin. Support for Labor is broad, but it is not deep.

Australian politics is changing faster than most political commentators can keep up with. The determination of independent MPs to insist that they aren't a party, the ability of the Greens to win and hold once-safe Liberal seats like Ryan, and the fact that there is no such thing as safe seats anymore all require a much more nuanced and humble analysis than the left/right/centre framing that has long dominated Australian political debate.

Now that neither the Liberal nor Labor party can afford to simply stay focused on each other anymore, lest their fight for traditional marginal seats cost them the once safest seats held by these most senior figures, and now that Labor, the Greens and progressive independents collectively hold 101 of the 150 seats in the lower house *and* a majority of the votes in the Senate, it is time to carefully consider what drives contemporary Australian politics and how that has changed. Australia clearly needs a new map to help navigate our rapidly changing political landscape.

Forging a new path

Australian electoral results put a hard edge on the woolly thinking behind the left/right/centre framework. While Labor's total of 94 seats in the 2025 House of Representatives election is remarkable, it is the collapse in both primary votes and lower house seats won by the Liberal Party that is more significant for those trying to project where Australia's democracy is heading. Landslides don't mean what they used to mean.

A government can pass as many laws with 76 voters in the House as it can with 94, but an opposition that has lost 34 seats in the last two elections is of no real threat at the next election, or likely the one after that. The weakness of the Liberals' primary vote and parliamentary representation will have more lasting consequences than Labor's parliamentary majority as it too is based on a very low primary vote. Put simply, while Labor has been picking up many of the seats the Liberals are losing, they are not picking up most of the voters the Liberals have been losing.

When Tony Abbott swept to victory in 2013, he won 90 seats, Labor held 55 and there was a crossbench of five. After the 2025 wipeout the Liberal and National parties now hold just 43 seats and the crossbench has largely held its own with 13 seats, with the most marginal seats held by both Labor and the Liberals vulnerable to independent candidates.

But despite the rising significance of both the number of three-cornered contests and the number of seats held by, or marginal to, independents and crossbenchers, the media's preferred metric for recording progress across the Australian electoral landscape, the two-party preferred vote, continues to elevate major parties and diminish all votes for minor parties and independents. Such a two-party centric map made sense 50 years ago, when the major parties won 95.8 per cent of the primary vote and the entirety of the lower house between them. But in 2025, when the two major parties between them managed just two thirds of the primary vote and lost one in ten seats to other candidates, such analysis hides the reality, and the vulnerability, of the major party performance.

Australia's major parties are lost in a democratic desert, shedding votes to new entrants faster than they can win them off each other. But the media's focus on the 2PP vote conceals how lost they are. Since the 1970s the bipartisan consensus to remain strategically silent about a wide range of issues, and in turn to avoid fights with powerful interests, has made governing easy but holding on to voters hard. For decades both major parties sought to avoid conflict with the Catholic Church, corporate Australia or countries like the United States about what being a good ally meant. As a result of the strategic silence of both "parties of government" about some of the biggest questions we face, Australian politics has revolved instead around having what look like big fights about relatively small things.

The rise of parties like the Greens and One Nation in the 1990s and the community independent movement more recently has led to open questioning of the shibboleths of the major party consensus, but to date the major parties seem more determined to hang on to the safety of the past than to hang on to their voters. Predictably, the legacy media that is losing audience even faster than the major parties are losing voters are the loudest voices urging the parties to ignore the siren song of voters demanding better and remain safely in the meaningless middle.[5] For example, Adelaide's *Advertiser* ran an editorial recommending a vote for either major party and against the "mad Greens, self-serving teals or the independent rabble". It's not clear why political parties seeking to win back voters should take advice from a media that can't win back readers.

The Coalition's irrelevance in the federal parliament is exacerbated by the fact that at the 2028 election Liberal and National candidates will simultaneously need to fight the Greens in seats like Ryan, teals in seats like Kooyong and Wentworth, Labor in seats like Sturt and Bullwinkel; and all while Liberal and National party candidates may end up fighting each other in seats like Bendigo and Grey. Even if the Coalition won back all the seats they lost to the left in the form of teal and Greens seats, then they would still need to win more than two dozen seats off Labor. In short, no government since the height of World War II has faced a less viable political threat from an opposition at the beginning of a parliamentary term than the Albanese Government in 2025.

But while the collapse in support for the Coalition should reduce fears among Labor MPs that they may lose office if they find their bravery, the media also needs to reconsider the veto they have long given to the Coalition over what constitutes sensible policy. Few with expertise in the Australian energy system, and seemingly few within the Coalition, ever took seriously the idea that a fleet of publicly owned nuclear power stations would be built by a Dutton government. But the norms of Australian politics meant that the media and the political class spoke (and are still speaking) as if those reactors were possible simply because a party of government had committed to them.

How many seats would the Coalition need to lose before they forfeit their ability to define what centrism in Australia means to the Australian media? If Senator Matt Canavan remains unconvinced that climate change is real, does that matter? Does the media have to host debates just because some people in parliament from a party that was once powerful still have strong feelings?

And just as importantly, for our parliament

and our public policy, if the Liberals and Nationals support Labor's approval of new coal and gas projects, can such bipartisan hostility to scientific evidence really be considered centrist? And if the Greens and independents think it's time for a public debate into gas and coal subsidies or bans on gambling advertising, will their priorities inevitably remain of less significance to the legacy media than the views of the Coalition?

Understanding how the Albanese Government conceives of centrism and uses it in parliament and in public debate will be critical to understanding how Labor uses the power it has recently been given by the electorate. Every time Labor introduces new legislation to the parliament they will face the same three options:

- Pass it with Greens support/amendments
- Pass it with Coalition support/amendments
- Fail to achieve change on the basis that it is better to do nothing than have the purity of their draft legislation contaminated by those constitutionally required to support new laws.

Bipartisan support is not a requirement of the Constitution, nor is it a requirement for longevity of legislation. Labor opposed the GST and John Howard's industrial relations policy WorkChoices, but all the former and much of the latter still remain law in Australia today. In enforcing the legislation, judges do not look back and see who voted for it.

In the last parliament the Albanese Government regularly argued that the Coalition had some form of veto power over a range of significant new laws including the creation of the National Anti-Corruption Commission (NACC), the reform of electoral funding laws and the creation of an Environmental Protection Authority. While some in the Labor Party may have been scarred by Tony Abbott's destruction of their policy initiatives a decade ago, the spectacular conflagration of that government in less than two years shows that even a forceful opponent can be a short-lived one.

Chasing approval from the conservative rump now left in parliament is not centrism and nor is it a good way to make policy. If Australia is to rapidly address crises such as climate change, inequality, Indigenous disadvantage and violence against women, then the current government, working with whatever votes it can muster in the Senate, needs to crack on and get things done. While some in Labor, including the prime minister, may prefer the symbolism of securing the Liberals' approval for his policy agenda, the problems facing the nation are too important to put the symbolism of who votes for change ahead of the urgency of the need for the change. As I mentioned before, John Howard didn't regret relying on Mal Colston to privatise Telstra, and nor did he regret agreeing to Bob Brown's demand for a ban on the construction of nuclear power stations in order to secure Greens support for an upgrade to the Lucas Heights nuclear reactor back in 1998.[6] Indeed, even during the 2025 election campaign, as Peter Dutton was struggling to explain why he wanted to build the nuclear power plants that John Howard himself had banned, the former prime minister offered no regrets:

> **Chris Kenny:** Now, energy is a massive issue in this campaign, a big challenge for the country — prices of electricity and security of supply. You're the

prime minister who did the deal with the Greens to outlaw domestic nuclear energy in this country. Was that a mistake? Do we need to fix it? And realistically, if any modern economy is going to cut their emissions to effectively zero, isn't nuclear energy imperative?

John Howard: Well, I can start with what we did some years ago. The reason I did that deal with the Greens and others was to get it through the Senate. I had to get through a piece of legislation that renewed the nuclear energy facility (which was vital to the treatment of certain forms of cancer) at Lucas Heights. Without that legislation, we'd have lost our nuclear medicine capacity, and why on earth the Labor Party thought it was helping the country to say, "No, we're not going to support you" ... So of course I sought refuge, much and all as I didn't like it, with the Greens and others. Now, was that a mistake then? I think in the context of the time, no. It was the only way we had of renewing the nuclear

> medicine facility. Now, of course it should be lifted; we should, and we have been advocating and very wisely asserting the need for nuclear power as part of the mix.[7]

John Howard didn't let the perfect be the enemy of the good, he didn't mind the optics of voting with the Greens, and he didn't even mind making small changes he disagreed with in order to secure bigger changes he thought important. And perhaps most importantly, he knew then and still knows now that a parliament can always come back and fix problems down the track if it wants to. In short, he knew his legacy as prime minister would be the things he changed, not the visibly valiant fights he had trying to change things.

To be clear, there is no right way for a parliament to make laws, and nor is there a right way for parliamentarians to behave in our parliamentary and public debates. It is culture, far more than our Constitution, which shapes the way our parliaments and our parliamentarians behave. Pretending your opponents can veto your reforms is entirely legal; it's just not something Hawke, Keating or Howard ever did.

Some maps are worse than others

No map is perfect, and all map-makers must decide what to leave out and what to highlight. Street directories are great for finding an address but terrible for finding a café that's open. Most world maps are Eurocentric and significantly exaggerate the physical size of countries near the poles (hint: Australia is more than three times the size of Greenland but on most maps, they look about the same size). And while Google Maps can include all sorts of real-time information, it is easy to manipulate. An artist once put 99 mobile phones in a child's toy wagon and walked up and down a quiet street causing the appearance of a traffic jam online and showing how anyone can divert traffic if they felt like it.[8]

Imperfect maps are unavoidable, but what is easy to avoid is overconfidence in the interpretation of any map, especially a map of something as complicated and as important as our democracy. If all maps are corruptible, then imagine what the most powerful companies in the world can do to manipulate a map of how our democracy works and our understanding of the importance of our votes, especially when those votes have the capacity to shape who gets billions each year in subsidies, whether enormously harmful new fossil fuel projects are approved and how much tax the wealthiest companies in the world will have to pay. If you were the CEO of a company that made billions selling the gas we gave you for free, wouldn't you spend a bit, or a lot, trying to ensure that no matter who won an election, no one asked you simple questions with embarrassing answers? Wouldn't you do all you could to convince voters they live in safe seats and that their votes don't really count? It is no accident the most powerful lobby groups mourn the decline of the primary vote of the parties of government and crave the certainty of majority government.

But the centrist map has not just distorted our view of which voters' voices matter; it has distorted our sense of what problems we are allowed to discuss and what solutions we are allowed to entertain. Allow me to demonstrate with three examples.

Climate science

The National Press Club once hosted a debate about the science of climate change between two non-scientists (I was one of them!) but it has never hosted a debate between epidemiologists and anti-vaxxers, or geologists and flat earthers. It is the distribution of political power, not the principles of centrism, which explains why the Australian media and political class facilitate the questioning of the science of climate change but not the science of vaccination or geology.

The fossil fuel industry is not just politically powerful enough to question science, it is politically powerful enough to be platformed by the Australian media and political class in order to disseminate its questioning of science. Indeed, it is so politically powerful that climate scientists and environmental groups carry the description "activist" or "extremist" while the CEOs of foreign-owned gas companies are "business leaders" and "job creators".

Once upon a time it was considered centrist

to include the tobacco industry in debates about the harms of smoking but luckily for subsequent generations, centrists are always willing to change their mind once the power has been shifted by others, and now big tobacco is not part of that conversation.

Carbon tax

Australians regularly hear that tax reform is critical for Australia's prosperity as well as goverments' ability to spend money on nice things. Australians hear that our tax system relies too heavily on income tax. And some Australians have come to believe we should embrace the advice of economists, even when those economists are advocating the pursuit of unpopular policies like increasing the GST. But when economists suggest taxing carbon pollution would be the most efficient way to tackle climate change, a proposition once publicly supported by John Hewson, John Howard, Tony Abbott, Malcolm Turnbull, Kevin Rudd, Julia Gillard, Bill Shorten and Anthony Albanese, we are now told such an idea is unworkable and unpopular. Apparently, it is centrist to support the unpopular ideas of economists when they profit powerful groups — such as company tax cuts, the privatisation of essential services, or the deregulation of companies with enormous market power such as the banks — but it is not centrist to support economic advice even when it is popular with the public if it offends powerful political groups like the fossil fuel industry.

AUKUS

While most Australians, and most political commentators, are somewhat cynical about the motives of Australian politicians, this cynicism often evaporates when there is bipartisan support for ideas that clearly benefit corporate or foreign power. For example, the AUKUS submarine project never went to Treasury or the Department of Foreign Affairs and Trade (DFAT) for detailed analysis before it was announced by Scott Morrison. Even though the then prime minister was not known for his attention to policy detail or commitment to long-term decision-making in the national interest, and even though the Albanese Labor opposition only had 24 hours to decide whether to support Australia's largest ever purchase, once there was bipartisan support the decision miraculously became sensible.

Most Labor or Coalition MPs know that the decision was made in a rush and is unlikely to result in Australia ever receiving the very expensive submarines, but that seems too cynical for centrists to even consider. The media is far more likely to ask critics of AUKUS what their plan is than they are to press the government on the complete lack of any contingency plan should the current or future US president become unwilling to sign over nuclear submarines to us at the time and price we are hoping for. Setting centrism up as a goal ignores the role played by those with the power to set the boundaries of what is sensible and what is extreme. Were the Greens or One Nation to suggest we make university or electricity free the media would be in an uproar about where the money would come from. But when both major parties commit to spending an extra $360 billion on defence the usual media obsession with fiscal responsibility and the need to restrain public spending simply evaporates. When Scott Morrison asked Josh Frydenberg whether Australia could afford the AUKUS price tag the then treasurer reportedly replied, “Everything is affordable if it’s a priority”.[9] And of course he is right. The truth of Australian politics is that once there is bipartisan support for a bad idea, the media will barely question it.

So, what would a centrist submarine policy look like? If Anthony Albanese decides to buy four nuclear submarines instead of six would that be a sensible shift towards the centre or a dangerous and expensive folly with Australia incurring all the risks of going nuclear and none of the benefits of having a large fleet? Or maybe we need seven? Luckily for centrists, the ALP and Coalition hastily agreed to six in the lead up to the 2022 election so there is no need to consider the fleet size at all. You can hide almost anything under the cloak of bipartisanship.

To be clear, this essay is not arguing against the need for parliamentarians to compromise, and nor is it arguing against the need for some policies that create change incrementally. Instead, the focus of this essay is on how unhelpful the left/right/centre framing is for a wide range of pressing issues. And relatedly, this essay is arguing that once you stop navigating as if all issues can be located on a left/right spectrum, the idea that a step towards the centre is always an improvement becomes meaningless.

Indeed, once people abandon the left/right/centre map it becomes far easier to spot when politicians are cynically picking policies and priorities purely to locate themselves in some imagined centre, and paint their opponents as extreme, in order to avoid genuine debate about the full range of available solutions. Better maps of our democracy help voters see for themselves how many paths we have available. Our current map often forces us to focus on whether we should simply press on further into the desert or go back to where we started. Just as there are now more than two parties, there are usually more than two policy paths to choose from.

If you ask a firefighter whether they would rather have a tanker full of water or nothing at all, they would likely agree that the tanker was better than nothing. That said, an aerial water bomber and a lot less climate change would make their task easier still. Skilled debaters know how to create binary choices with only one sensible option, but it is dangerous to conclude that all steps in the right direction get us closer to victory. For a small fire, a bucket of water might be all that's needed, but it's dangerous folly to suggest that those asking if we need more firefighting aircraft instead of more buckets are letting the perfect be the enemy of the good.

Subsidising new solar panels is obviously a step towards a lower carbon energy market, but if such a step conceals the government's ongoing subsidisation of large 4WDs (the most common vehicles on our roads), their subsidies for diesel used in mining (one of the largest users of liquid fuels) or the subsidisation of exploration for as-yet-undiscovered deposits of coal and reservoirs of gas then is it at all meaningful to ask, stripped of all context, whether the solar panels are a step in the right direction or not? Framing clever questions is a lot easier than solving big problems.

Is it churlish to criticise a government for doing harmful things on the basis that they did a good thing too? Is it cynical to think that governments would use a small step in one policy domain (such as solar) to conceal much larger steps in others (such as approving the North West Shelf gas extension)? And is it centrist to focus on the good news while ignoring the economic waste and inefficiency of a government that is simultaneously subsidising both fossil fuels *and* renewable energy? Is it centrist to evaluate each small policy in isolation; or is it okay for centrists to evaluate the full suite of policies to see if they work in concert or in conflict with each other?

Compromise and incrementalism have key roles to play in democracies, but a naïve adherence to centrism sheds no light on who is setting the boundaries for debate and conceals the compromises politicians agree to make with one another about which fights to have and which ones to dodge.

When a person, a party, or a country makes it clear that it will always be willing to compromise then it will always fall victim to those who insist they will not give an inch. Indeed, once someone declares they will always be happy to meet others in the middle they give their opponents an incentive to drive a hard bargain.

Centrism and the fight for what is right

In the fight against slavery, abolitionists eventually prevailed over slave owners. The long fight was not won in the sensible centre, but by "radical, democratic" absolutists who risked their lives in the fight to save the lives of others.[10] It scares me to think how the ABC, or indeed most of the world's media, would report on such a debate today. Can you imagine the economic modelling on the jobs that would be lost in the slave-using industries? Or the endless discussion of the impact on the price of clothes if slaves didn't pick cotton? And can you imagine the modern debate about the best way to compensate hard-working slave owners whose business model was based on long-accepted rules allowing whipping and branding? Slavery persists today, and England (the major global slave trader of the 1800s) paid out the equivalent of over £17 billion in compensation to slave owners in 1837, but it's important to remember that change was driven by abolitionists, not centrists. The incrementalism on the path to abolition was a consequence of sustained pressure against change, but the incrementalism was never the goal. Unsurprisingly, few mock the extremism of those who fought to end slavery in the US and UK, and few argue abolitionists would have achieved more if they had asked for less.

Leaders such as António Guterres, the Secretary-General of the UN, have long been arguing for immediate and decisive action on climate both for existential and moral reasons.[11] He is not interested in a middle ground. The climate science says time is crucial. For those determined to avoid dangerous climate change the goal isn't to decarbonise the economy, but to decarbonise it before scientific thresholds are reached. It is physics that says we will melt the ice caps, raise sea levels radically and warm waters so much that we don't just kill the Great Barrier Reef, but we will kill whole food systems in our oceans and on our farmlands. You either accept the physics or you don't but committing to the goal of decarbonising and not committing to the physics-imposed deadlines is like committing to stopping smoking after you have your second heart attack.

The science says we do need to rush. It is now over 30 years since the Australian government first accepted that climate change was real, was primarily caused by fossil fuels, and was an enormous risk to Australia, but centrists like Albanese are still telling us that it's not yet time to stop building new gas or coal mines. Saying those who accept climate science are extreme when they call for more ambitious and urgent action is like criticising a drowning man for being impatient about the delay in launching a rescue boat. Timing is critical for some problems and solving them too late isn't a solution at all.

Scientific evidence simply doesn't recognise political pragmatism or positioning, but while many political centrists express support for evidence-based policy, in reality when the evidence and politics clash centrists usually support the politics, often on the basis that something is better than nothing or that the perfect should not be the enemy of the good.

António Guterres is clearly an extremist by Australian standards when he says, "We are hurtling towards disaster, eyes wide open … It's time to wake up and step up … leave oil, coal and gas in the ground where they belong."[12] But does anyone think he would change his comments if he knew that Labor had more ambitious household battery policies than the Coalition?

Scientific evidence, cost-benefit analyses, opinion polling and principled leadership all have a role to play in driving reforms. But while each of these ingredients can play an important role in shaping policy, the ultimate shape of policy, and the public's reaction to it, will be determined by the judgement and political skill of those in power and their ability to align their priorities with those of the community they wish to serve.

In Australia centrism means that it's okay to ignore evidence if the other side ignores it too.

Centrism and a captured media

According to some in the legacy Australian media, The Australia Institute is a "left-wing think tank" (we prefer "progressive") with vested interests and anti-gas views. According to that same media, the CEOs of foreign-owned companies are simply well-respected captains of industry, business leaders and job creators whose main goal is to grow the Australian economy and pay taxes that support Australian schools and hospitals.

While I personally don't mind if the media calls me left wing (I certainly think inequality and climate change are bad, and I certainly think publicly run health and education systems are better than privatised ones) I am confused why some in the media feel obliged to describe me as an "activist" just because I am an economist opposed to public subsidies for foreign-owned companies selling a polluting product. I'm also confused why they introduce the proponents of those mines and gas wells — paid representatives of companies that receive public funding (sometimes paying zero tax) — as neutral experts.

Welcome to the topsy-turvy world of the Australian media.

Of course, the legacy media's difficulty in navigating Australia's rapidly changing political landscape goes much deeper than their struggles with who to talk to and how to describe them. For decades the legacy media has earnestly reported on what the government of the day, and the opposition of the day, thought about the issues that the government or opposition had decided were important. But now that more people vote for crossbenchers than the Coalition, how should the legacy media decide what issues are politically important?

Consider the following: if most Australians think gambling advertising is a big problem, but neither party wants to talk about it, is the lack of response from the government and the opposition proof that gambling is not a story or proof that both major parties are at odds with the vast majority of voters?

Most Australian journalists and their editors

follow the agenda set by politicians. This dynamic helps explain why the major political parties' vote share and the circulation of newspapers are both in steady decline. While it is the role of the government and opposition to debate their respective parliamentary agendas, it is the role of a well-functioning media not only to cover the content of those debates, but also to critique where necessary that debate. You might think the fact that neither major party wants to unpack AUKUS or how a country that has tripled gas exports in the last ten years could possibly have a shortage of gas should be a big story.[13] Instead, most of the legacy media interpret the refusal of senior politicians to talk about important issues as proof that they are simply not a story.

The ABC is still using an old map which means that while only 318,000 people subscribe to *The Australian*[14], *The Australian*'s editors know that their front pages can set the agenda for the ABC and other outlets. Likewise, while only 40,000 of Australia's 15 million voters watch Sky News each night, its producers know their job is to shift the boundaries of public debate which is much easier than shifting the minds of all those participating in it. This past election showed that, more than ever before, legacy media holds little sway with the voting public, but they still play a major role in deciding which voices and which ideas are sensible and which are extreme.

Bipartisan silence on an issue may be proof that current policy settings are located comfortably in the sensible centre, based on solid evidence and with broad community support. Australia's continued reliance on 240v electricity, driving on the left side of the road and our ban on privately owned assault rifles would all fit that bill. But bipartisan refusal to question whether subsidies for private schools have improved Australia's education system or whether fossil fuel subsidies deliver good value for Australian taxpayers more likely reflect the desire of both major parties to conceal the strength of their support for powerful groups. And media silence on issues the major parties choose to ignore only further entrenches voter disaffection with the political and commentator class.

The risks of centrism in a broad church

The Australian Labor Party is as much a broad church as John Howard once proclaimed the Liberal Party to be. The Labor Party contains multitudes, from conservative Catholics who openly opposed same-sex marriage to openly gay and now legally married members; free marketeers and staunch interventionists; budget hawks and proud Keynesians; and of course, those who accept the science of climate change and those desperate to drive fossil fuel expansion. Disagreements about principles, policies and political strategy are common in any large group, but what matters for the country is not that differences of opinion exist in a party, but how a party manages those differences. Unfortunately, in Australia, the credo that division is death is so widely accepted across all of our political parties that the media treats the mere whiff of public difference of opinion not as inevitable, or even healthy, but toxic.

Australian parliaments are dominated by strict party discipline. This was on display when Senator Fatima Payman crossed the floor, voting against a Labor decision not to recognise Palestine. This led to her leaving the Labor Party. The ALP is particularly rigid when it comes to the requirement of all its MPs to vote for the party position all of the time. Elsewhere in parliament while crossing the floor to vote against your party is permitted by the Liberals, the Nationals, One Nation and the Greens it is by far the exception rather than the norm.

Crossing the floor is deeply discouraged in Australian parliamentary culture, and sometimes even a sackable offence, but that is not the case in most parliaments around the world. The so-called Westminster system is not based on binding bloc voting and those elected to Congress in the US vote according to their personal views rather than the party line so often that there isn't even a widely used term for the practice. They simply think of it as voting.

While uncommon around the world, binding all members of a political party to vote as a bloc, as instructed by the party leadership, has several advantages for a political party, and especially for its leaders. Indeed, bloc voting likely has some benefits for voters, who instead of taking the time to get to know the principles, priorities and policies of those aspiring to be their local member in the House of Representatives, can simply listen to what the prime minister or opposition say and then trust their local MP will vote as instructed. But there are costs to such an approach to party discipline.

All MPs get a voice in their party room debates about policy and priorities, but once a party room decision is made, all voices support it as one, whether they believe in it or not. In turn, when you hear a minister mounting a passionate defence of their party's position on why it is irresponsible to increase unemployment benefits, good for the climate to expand gas and coal production, or responsible for Australia to rely on Donald Trump and all future US presidents to honour the terms of our AUKUS alliance, you have no idea if the minister actually believes a word they are saying or not. The minister with the loudest voice supporting a position may well have led the charge against it in the party room and the cabinet.

While political autobiographies are full of former politicians telling of their private bravery, and no doubt the coming decades will be full of mea culpas from MPs wishing their private urgings had delivered more to tackle Indigenous disadvantage, rising inequality and climate change, Australian political culture means that those in power are not just required to vote for legislation they oppose, but to publicly attack advocates they agree with.

Some may remember that Paul Keating once failed to convince his party to adopt a GST and then proudly destroyed John Hewson's proposal to deliver Keating's preferred tax reform. Peter Garrett once ran as a candidate for the Nuclear Disarmament Party but subsequently made the case for the expansion of uranium mining when he was a Labor minister. In the words of Kevin Rudd,

> Any political party ... contains within it a whole range of views which we formalise through democratic processes ... And guess what? Not everyone always gets their own way — I don't get my way on everything — I understand that. Therefore, it is our job, however, to take

> our unified message out to the Australian people.[15]

Peter Garrett subsequently wrote that supporting Rudd was the biggest mistake he made in his political career.[16]

And more recently, Senator Penny Wong spent years strongly arguing against the right of same-sex couples to marry, including on the basis that "cultural, religious, historical view … this is an institution that is between a man and a woman".[17]

To be clear, when Penny Wong told us she opposed same-sex marriage she was doing her job of supporting current Labor policy whether she supports it or not, a job she clearly doesn't resile from. When Senator Fatima Payman quit the Labor Party on the basis she could not vote against a motion supporting Palestine, Senator Wong said, "We understand the importance of caucus solidarity. It is very rare for a Labor person not to respect that. It's a principle which has served us well."[18]

The problem is not that politicians openly support policies that they disagree with and attack advocates outside their party they do agree with, it's that our public debate takes the arguments, and attacks made on others, seriously. To be clear, at the same time centrists in the media and pragmatists in NGOs are supporting government policies as the best available option, some of the ministers promoting those same policies, and mocking those with greater ambition, will almost inevitably have spoken against those same ideas in the party room and in cabinet. How can we have serious debates about important issues when many of those involved are obliged to keep their thoughts to themselves and demean those they agree with?

No wonder people are losing faith in democracy. We have built a system where party control supersedes personal conscience, and worse, a system where those MPs who are seen to have integrity on an issue are more likely to be used as battering rams against their external allies while privately supporting ideas and values they publicly deride.

It is no coincidence that the number of Australians voting for independents and minor parties is rising so rapidly. The problem for major parties is not that their candidates are bad people. The problem is that, given the option of representatives who simply parrot the party line and those who can say what they genuinely believe and vote according to their conscience on every issue, voters are increasingly choosing independents. The problems for major parties are particularly acute when they try to convert questions of morality into a centrist compromise. While moral gymnastics and strict adherence to agreed talking points might keep a large party room together, such centrist compromising often leaves voters cold.

Party leaders understand how insincere and unpersuasive such compromises can be, which is why both major parties often work together to keep issues such as same-sex marriage out of parliament. The same is true today for issues like gambling and fossil fuel expansion and the taxation of churches; those in parliament know that any compromise position that a large party room can agree to will likely appear unpersausive to those outside parliament. It's not just lobbyists that stop parliament debating important issues, it is the desire of the major parties to maintain the appearance of cohesion on issues that they know divide them.

Minor parties and independent MPs allow

issues that the major parties dare not speak of to be discussed openly and even debated in parliament, which helps explain the venom that is often directed towards them by major party MPs.

Emissions evasions

While for the past 15 years the Labor Party has adopted more ambitious domestic emissions reduction targets than the Coalition, this has not always been the case. At the 1990 federal election, Andrew Peacock promised a "fair go for the environment" including reductions in greenhouse gas emissions by 20 per cent by the year 2000.[19] Three years later, John Hewson's Fightback! package retained that commitment.[20] Both men failed to lead their side to victory, but nobody argued, then or later, that it was because of their emissions reduction pledges. Just as climate change isn't a left-wing issue in Europe, it didn't even use to be a left-wing issue in Australia.

The Albanese Government's current domestic emissions reduction targets are unrelated to the science of limiting dangerous climate change to just 1.5°C. Indeed, Labor's current targets are inconsistent with our international obligations under the Paris Agreement. But, while inconsistent with keeping Australia safe or meeting our international commitments, it is easy for commentators to focus on the fact that Labor's targets are better than the Coalition position. If only atmospheric physics responded to centrist political positioning, we'd be heading for an ice age.

Labor relies heavily on the fact that the 43 per cent domestic emissions target it legislated after the 2022 election was more ambitious than the Liberals wanted and less ambitious than the Greens' target[21] — such positioning on targets, be they emissions, renewable energy, electric cars or any other green thing is the easiest way for Labor to prove their policy ambition is in the sensible centre while simultaneously picking fights with the Liberals and the Greens on the basis that they are extreme. But can you imagine political parties setting blood-alcohol limits for drivers in this way, or the safe level of exposure to lead?

In order to hold its party room together, Labor leaders work hard to transform binary issues of right and wrong into a left/right spectrum on which they can locate themselves in the sensible centre. And just as the issue of same-sex marriage caused internal angst and a loss of external credibility, the issue of fossil fuel expansion causes similar problems. To date Labor has managed to convince itself, most of the media, and a lot of voters, that because their position on domestic renewables is more ambitious than the Liberals' their ongoing support for gas and coal mining makes them "centrist". But the hardening science, the growing cost of extreme weather, and shifting public awareness mean that the current centre is unlikely to hold.

Australia is already one of the world's largest fossil fuel exporters, and all climate scientists agree that for fossil fuel emissions to reduce, the world needs to burn far less fossil fuel. And no matter where in the world our coal or gas is burned, it will harm Australia's climate.

But because the decision to stop approving new gas and coal projects is a binary choice, Labor cannot do its preferred kind of centrism and choose a percentage that fits between the Greens and the Liberals. To date their most effective strategy is to simply avoid the question, a strategy made easy by a proudly centrist media.

There is no science that says modest growth

in fossil fuel production is safe for the climate. Put another way, only those willing to deny climate science can support the expansion of fossil fuels, or even the continuation of the current rate of fossil fuel production, at this point in history. So how does Labor manage to seem centrist in its support for climate action while enthusiastically approving and subsidising new fossil fuel projects and publicly funding exploration for new, as yet undiscovered, deposits of gas and coal?

Sadly, it's quite easy.

Labor's first line of centrist defence against the consensus of climate science is to take the simple scientific proposition that it is unsafe to continue to expand fossil fuel production and restate it as the need to instantly close all gas and coal mines tomorrow. Leaving aside that I have never heard anyone call for the instant closure of all Australian fossil fuel projects, Labor MPs have spent more than a decade ruling out any willingness to take an extreme step no one has called on them to take.

The following lengthy extract shows how much work goes into thinking up ways to avoid simple questions about why a country that is transitioning away from fossil fuels needs to produce more fossil fuels. It's not easy to read but that's the point. Boring people is key to the strategy of distracting them from the simple truth.

> **Patricia Karvelas:** Okay, last time we spoke I asked you a question and a lot of my listeners were concerned that you didn't answer it, so I'm going to ask it again in this interview. It's like an ongoing conversation we're having. Why do we need new coal and gas?

> **Chris Bowen:** Well, what we need is a sensible — saying "no new coal and gas" is, frankly, a slogan, not a policy. What we need is a sensible transition to a much more renewable economy. So, let's just take the National Energy Grid for example, and then I'll deal with manufacturing. But the National Energy Grid, Patricia, we're going to get it to 82 per cent renewable by 2030. That's 82 months away. It's a huge task, a big lift. It'll still mean that of the 82 per cent renewable, 18 per cent will be non-renewable. That means you've got

to have supply. You've got to have the supply —

…

Chris Bowen: You've got gas fields, you know, with reducing production in the southern states, for example. We need to ensure that the gas-fired power stations have supply and that's before we even get to manufacturing for which green hydrogen will step forward and I'm very confident will replace natural gas, but it's not there yet and it's several years away. So, we've got to get this transition right. It's all very well, with due respect to the Greens, for them to say, "We want this, and we want that." Our job is to manage this transition —

…

Chris Bowen: Well, with respect, Patricia, you've got the ACCC, AEMO pointing to gas shortages at various points. Yes, we've got to manage the export market. A lot of this has already been contracted. You can't disturb that. You've also got to manage the ADGSM, the gas Code of Conduct. All that we have in place. All that we have in place.

...

Chris Bowen: It would be irresponsible, Patricia — let me make it very clear, as the Prime Minister's saying in a speech this morning: gas has a role to play for peaking and firming for many years to come. It would be irresponsible to put some sort of blanket ban on as we are undertaking this massive transition, coming after ten years of denial and delay, starting in 2022 to get a 2030 target. Yes, it's ambitious and difficult and complicated.

Patricia Karvelas: ... Don't we have enough gas?

Chris Bowen: Well, that's, with respect, that's not quite right. What we did was put a gas supply — or a gas price cap on in December, with the support of the Greens and the crossbench, which we acknowledge and appreciate. No support from the opposition. But it does not provide an opportunity for the Parliament or the government to go in and cancel export contracts and nor should it. There'd be constitutional issues, there'd be sovereign risk issues, there'd be trade issues. What we've got to do is, I'm very keen to ensure that we have as much domestic gas supply as is necessary and possible, of course. That means we have to have difficult conversations with gas companies, which we've had, about the Code of Conduct, about ADGSM and the trigger.

…

Chris Bowen: I'm suggesting, Patricia — I've said it now, I think, six or seven times — it would be irresponsible to have a blanket ban. I've said that consistently from the beginning. That has been our position in the private conversation with

> Bandt. It's been our position publicly. And Bandt's position has been the same privately as publicly. That's their view. But it's an offer not an ultimatum. He's happy to have good faith talks. We've had those, and we'll continue to have them.

Still awake? See how Minister Bowen doesn't mention coal at all? See how he talks about domestic renewables and domestic demand for gas? To be fair, Patricia Karvelas did a good job of showing her listeners that he simply can't explain why his government is still approving new gas and coal mines. But the caravan moves on. Bowen hasn't been asked such simple questions since.

Anthony Albanese was recently asked why his government just approved a 45-year extension for Woodside's gas export project on the North West Shelf 1500 km north of Perth. His answer revolved around the need for an aluminium smelter in the New South Wales Hunter Valley to have a reliable electricity supply. There is no pipeline connecting Woodside's gas export facility to New South Wales, but no journalist pointed that out. That wouldn't be polite.

Having knocked down the straw man argument of how reckless it would be to instantly shut down all fossil fuel projects and break all the contracts that fossil fuel companies have signed, Labor's next centrist defence is to ignore the question of "why are you ignoring science and approving new fossil fuels" and answer the unasked question of what are you doing on renewable energy?

That is, rather than explain their ongoing support for fossil fuel expansion, Labor MPs have been trained to talk instead about the amount of renewable energy they are supporting in the domestic economy. A focus on renewable energy allows Labor spokespeople to highlight that they are taking action on climate change while placing themselves in the sensible centre between the Liberals who are less supportive of — and often hostile to — renewable energy on one end of the spectrum and the Greens who (allegedly) want to shut down all the mines tomorrow at the other end.

To be clear, investing in renewable energy is a good idea, and Labor policy has driven a lot more of it than the Coalition, but just as taking the doctor's advice to walk more and ignoring their advice to stop smoking isn't an evidence-based or centrist approach to healthcare, supporting renewable energy while subsidising new fossil fuel projects is not a solution to keep Australians safe from dangerous climate change.

The question of why both major political parties are so supportive of the fossil fuel industry and other extractive industries, including the tiny industries of native forest logging and salmon farming, needs an essay in itself. Suffice it to say that most resource ministers wind up working for the resource industry, and resource ministers clearly see their role as being a voice for resource companies rather than a voice for the Australians who own those resources. No resource minister in modern history has interpreted their role as maximising the economic benefits of Australian resources for Australian voters, preferring instead to interpret their role as representing the needs and interests of foreign-owned resources companies. Of course it is prime ministers who appoint our resource ministers.

Peter Dutton's desperation for votes led him to speak the unspeakable truth during the 2025 election when he stated Australia didn't have a shortage of gas and that we were simply exporting too much of it. In all likelihood, his successors and the Labor Party will work hard to suggest no such statement was ever made. Winners write history, and like Labor's former support for a carbon tax, Dutton's statement that Australia doesn't have a gas shortage will likely disappear from view, at least if the gas industry gets it way.

Australia is now the second largest exporter of fossil fuels in the world and planning a massive expansion in gas and coal exports even though we are, allegedly, 30 years into our decarbonisation of the economy. Again, no one need fear we will rush into anything extreme.

National Anti-Corruption Commission

Kevin Rudd, Julia Gillard and, once upon a time, Anthony Albanese, were all once opposed to the need for a federal anti-corruption commission, primarily on the basis that there was no evidence such a body was needed. Recent events revealed the folly of that position. But as recently as 2015, Gary Gray, a former Labor Minister for Resources who worked for Woodside before entering parliament, and a mining company after leaving parliament, declared that:

> An ICAC-type body is needed where there is a lack of institutions to protect the integrity of public processes and the public interest. This is not the case federally.

> Although the need for an ICAC-type body has been discussed for 30 years, the ALP has always rejected a federal ICAC while supporting and reviewing existing integrity measures.[22]

Perhaps unsurprisingly, a number of Labor frontbenchers suggested the creation of a federal corruption watchdog would need bipartisan support, even though there has long been sufficient crossbench support for a major party to create such a body if they wished. Tellingly, Gary Gray gave an insight into how much major parties cooperated in the past on potentially embarrassing issues, as in the past when it came to examining each other's travel expenses both major parties had decided to call a truce:

> the whole idea of politicians being able to travel to their work was coming under question. We agreed to stop using entitlements as part of the general warfare in political parties, except where there was clear and genuine abuse.[23]

The problem for centrists is that it was once considered extreme to suggest that corruption existed in federal politics. Of course it was possible to interpret the bipartisan hostility to the creation of a federal anti-corruption watchdog as evidence that no such body was necessary, and indeed when The Australia Institute's research began to highlight the need for a federal anti-corruption watchdog back in 2015 a surprising range of NGOs shared the assessment that since it was impossible to create such a body no one should even discuss it: the idea alone, we were told, would distract attention from smaller but more achievable goals.

Despite bipartisan hostility, and apathy among many NGOs, the first poll conducted by The Australia Institute on the issue in 2016 showed 65 per cent public support for a federal ICAC.[24] One of the most common misunderstandings of Australian politics is the belief that politicians are poll driven and will only do things that are popular to the exclusion of things that are hard. In reality, cracking down on corruption, abolishing gambling advertising, curbing fossil fuel subsidies and making the gas industry pay more tax are all overwhelmingly popular. It takes resolve and determination for our political leaders to resist such popular public interest policy. Again, this is why the biggest corporate lobbyists feel so hostile to the smallest political parties and independents since they reveal the old tricks of bipartisanship.

One of the key goals of a think tank is to make the radical seem reasonable, and it is often hard for people to believe how often, and how quickly, such political transformations take place. In turn, many were surprised that as soon as then Opposition Leader Bill Shorten announced in 2018 at the National Press Club that a Labor government would create a National Integrity Commission that then PM Malcolm Turnbull declared he was open to the idea. Visible bipartisan hostility had transformed into visible bipartisan willingness to change in just hours.[25]

Even after Malcolm Turnbull lost the prime ministership and Bill Shorten lost the 2019 election — both to Scott Morrison — the bipartisan support for a federal corruption watchdog remained intact. While it had been convenient for both parties to ignore the need for a watchdog for decades, now that such a body could no longer be dismissed as extreme neither party wanted to be first to renege on the commitment to create one.

Unfortunately, one of the most dangerous things in politics is when powerful people agree with you in principle and do nothing in practice. Bluff bills put up to fail are among the most cynical of political tricks, but old-fashioned efforts at dragging your feet can be highly effective. And so it was with Scott Morrison who, having won the miracle election in 2019 and having committed in principle to the creation of an anti-corruption commission, subsequently voted against a Greens bill to create such a body and refused to propose one of his own. Significantly, with Labor in opposition at the time, and keen to put as much pressure on the Liberals as possible, Anthony Albanese's party voted in 2021 for a Greens bill to create a national integrity commission with real teeth, including the power to hold public hearings whenever it was in the public interest to do so.[26] Clearly the Greens and Labor can work together when they want to.

After Labor won the 2022 election, however, the desire for centrism trumped the desire to show the public that Labor was more concerned with the issue than Morrison's Liberal Party. Despite Labor having voted for the Greens' proposed corruption watchdog in 2019, and despite the fact that Labor had publicly supported the role of public hearings for such a watchdog, when it came time for Labor to secure the passage of what we now know as the National Anti-Corruption Commission (NACC) through the parliament they chose to negotiate not with the Greens or independents who were enthusiastic about the idea, but with the Liberals who were apathetic at best. In turn both major parties agreed, behind closed doors, to only allow public hearings in exceptional circumstances.[27]

So, what is centrist when it comes to corruption watchdogs? Was it centrist of the major parties to agree that no such body was needed at a federal level? Was it centrist for Labor to support public hearings when they were in opposition and looking to embarrass the Liberals? Or was it centrist for both major parties to deliver in principle on the creation of a watchdog which, in practice, has disappointed all of those who worked for a decade to create it?

While symbolism matters in politics, what matters most is that when Labor had the choice to work with the crossbench or the Coalition to pass the NACC through parliament, it clearly preferred to work with the less ambitious and more conservative block of Coalition votes in the Senate.

Fair electoral reforms

Clive Palmer spent $123 million campaigning against Labor during the 2022 election.[28] And in the lead up to the referendum on an Indigenous Voice to Parliament the dangers of a misleading scare campaign from the No campaign were nearly as high for Anthony Albanese as they were for the Indigenous Australians who had risked so much to ask for so little from the Australian people.

The devastating referendum result and Clive Palmer's expenditure of a further $60 million during the 2025 election, combined with the rise of AI and deepfakes in advertising, show how urgent, and important, electoral law reform should have been for the Albanese Government's first term.[29] But that is clearly not how Labor saw things.

Rather than work with the Greens and crossbench to draft and pass legislation to require truth in political advertising (such as the laws that exist in the ACT and South Australia), to limit the ability of Clive Palmer and Liberal-linked campaigners Advance to produce misleading political ads, Labor instead chose to defer to the priorities of the Coalition (a grouping of four separate parties) on the basis of the "centrality of the two-party system".

In choosing to delay the introduction of electoral reforms until after the referendum, Labor gave a significant advantage to those who were determined to mislead voters. In choosing to negotiate with the Liberals, rather than the Greens or independents, in the months leading up to the introduction of the Electoral Reform Bill, Labor was choosing to protect the ability of the Cormack Foundation (part-owned by the Liberal Party) to make unlimited donations to the Liberal Party. At the same time, they were choosing to work with the Liberals in designing a system that would support incumbent parties and MPs, while making it harder for new parties or new independents to raise and spend money from the 2028 election onwards.

So willing was Labor to work with the Coalition that they weakened their own bargaining position. As Paul Karp wrote when the bill was delayed after Dutton played hardball, "The special minister of state, Don Farrell, did not do enough to keep the crossbench pathway alive, giving the Coalition too much leverage to demand changes on donation limits and disclosure thresholds."[30] Indeed, the final laws that passed looked more like a Coalition wish-list than Labor policy.

Shortly before the 2025 federal election landslide, Labor Senator for the ACT Katy Gallagher was asked whether Labor would pursue the issue of increased Senate representation for Canberrans. The *Senate (Representation of Territories) Act 1973* rather than the Constitution stipulates the ACT has two senators compared with Tasmania's 12. Senator Gallagher's response was as revealing as it was disheartening for the majority of voters who chose not to vote for the Liberals at this year's election. She said:

> when you're making big changes it's no good if you've got, you know, a major part of the political spectrum saying no and politicising it, you saw what happened in the referendum. I don't think that's sensible in electoral reform, which is why we would hope that in another term that

> the Liberal Party might consider that as something Canberra needs as opposed to what [the Liberal Party] need.[31]

So, no reform until the Liberals decide not to politicise things …

According to polling by The Australia Institute, there is strong public support for laws to require truth in political advertising (89 per cent[32]) and strong support for electoral laws that make it easier for new parties and independents to run for parliament (67 per cent[33]). Likewise, it is hard to see how issues of honesty, fair political playing fields or the principle of equal representation are in any way left wing; indeed they would seem to be quite conservative in the historical sense of the word. But that's not where our current democratic map locates them.

In short, Labor's stated preference for bipartisanship clearly has nothing to do with philosophical centrism. On the contrary, the stated preference for bipartisanship on a wide range of issues is little more than a polite way to conceal a simple truth: when Labor doesn't want to do something progressive it simply asks the Liberals for permission, knowing they will be rebuffed.

The exception that tests the rule: industrial relations reform

As I've mentioned, John Howard didn't seek bipartisan support before introducing the GST, privatising Telstra, joining the US invasion of Iraq or passing WorkChoices through the parliament with a slim majority. Likewise, Tony Abbott didn't ask Labor if they would mind if he abolished the carbon tax that Julia Gillard had successfully negotiated with the Greens and other crossbenchers.

When it is serious about passing legislation, Labor does not ask for permission from the Coalition. The clearest evidence for this comes from Labor's successful approach to legislating significant industrial relations (IR) reforms after their narrow 2022 election victory. Put simply, as the Albanese Government was serious about achieving IR reform, as opposed to serious about positioning themselves as centrist and blaming the Greens and Coalition for any lack of progress, Labor was happy to negotiate with the Greens and crossbench to secure their support. There was no chest-thumping about mandates, nor was there blanket hostility to suggested amendments. On the contrary, Labor was happy to use the Greens to strengthen worker rights even further than they had promised during the 2022 election campaign.

In October 2022, the Albanese Government introduced its "Secure Jobs, Better Pay" legislation that promised to expand "access to single and multi-employer bargaining", cap fixed-term contracts at two years, and abolish the Australian Building and Construction Commission and the Registered Organisations Commission.[34] The legislation passed through both the House and the Senate with the Greens and David Pocock providing the necessary votes in the Senate; the Liberals and Nationals voted against it.

Significantly, in March 2023, the Greens introduced a "Right to Disconnect" private members' bill, but it was subsequently removed from the notice paper. Labor and the Greens then agreed to include a version of the Greens' proposed reform in the "Closing Loopholes Bill

No. 2", which passed in early 2024.[35] In addition to legislating the Greens' proposal the "Closing Loopholes" bill promised to "properly define casual work" and "criminalise wage theft", "prevent labour hire from being used to undercut agreed rates of pay" and better regulate "silica safety and silica-related diseases". As with the "Secure Jobs, Better Pay" legislation the "Closing Loopholes" bill passed the House and Senate (despite opposition from the Coalition) with support from the Greens and Senators David Pocock and Lidia Thorpe.

Last term, the Albanese Government made clear that it is willing and able to legislate significant reforms even when the Coalition was opposed. And likewise, they demonstrated that, when they are serious about the passage of legislation, they are willing and able to negotiate with the Greens and other senators to include provisions in bills that strengthen legislation beyond what had originally been promised. In the case of the NACC, Labor showed they are willing to weaken legislation and in turn do less than they promised. In each case it is a choice.

The choice made by the government of the day about which path, if any, they seek through the Senate is one of the most important but least discussed issues in Australian politics. John Howard was happy to water down the GST to get it through the Senate with Democrat support; Malcolm Turnbull was willing to negotiate with the Greens to reform the way we elect senators. Negotiating with the Senate is hardly a new or extreme idea.

Using the refusal of your political rivals to pass your legislation is a great way to get media and a terrible way to get change. If the Albanese Government is willing to treat the inequality, climate and Indigenous disadvantage crises as seriously as it took IR reform during the last term, then it will quickly become one of the most reforming governments in Australian history. Who said politics is boring?

Rethinking Australian politics

The terms "prime minister", "opposition leader", "mandate" and "bluff bill" are not mentioned in our Constitution. Until an amendment in 1977, our founding democratic document didn't even mention political parties, and that amendment only clarifies how the parliament should replace a retiring senator. Nor is there anything in our Constitution, or our history, that says good policy requires bipartisan consensus. But in recent decades, as our political culture has circled around the drain of centrism, promising much, delivering little and undermining the public's faith in the power of government to make our lives better, bipartisanship has replaced bravery and boldness for many in power as the mark of good policy and good politics. But there are few battles you can win by avoiding conflict and demanding consensus.

Bob Hawke had no mandate for his biggest

changes and didn't even mention his plans to float the dollar during the 1983 election campaign. There was no economic modelling of the costs and benefits of that decision. In fact, some ministers had no idea of the significance of what Hawke had decided to do until they read about it in the newspapers the next day. Likewise, Scott Morrison cooked up Australia's part in AUKUS with no input from Treasury or DFAT. Straight after the 2022 election campaign, the Albanese Government announced a $1.5 billion subsidy for the Middle Arm gas project in Darwin Harbour despite never mentioning the project during the election. Julia Gillard created the National Disability Insurance Scheme and Scott Morrison spent $267 billion on COVID stimulus. When asked about the Coalition's COVID spending John Howard advised Josh Frydenberg that there were "no ideological constraints" in times of crisis.[36] Australian leaders know how to make big decisions and write big cheques when they want to.

But while ramming historic legislation through parliament is the stuff political histories are made of, the reality in modern Australia is that our major political parties put significant effort into picking fake fights, and drafting bluff bills, to create the appearance of drive and determination, so they can conceal their apathy, fear of upsetting corporate interests and desire to conceal internal division. While it is rarely discussed, in Australia the best way to justify inaction is to self-identify as a sensible centrist who just can't get those other nasty parties to support change. Those who profit from the status quo foment the idea that big changes require bipartisan consensus.

Professional politicians know how little attention most Australians pay to legislation passing through parliament. Indeed, most politicians know that they themselves read few, if any, of the laws they vote on. And when most people don't care about most of the laws debated in parliament the main task of the government of the day is to attract as much attention as they can to the fights they want people to see and as little attention as possible for the things they, and often the opposition, are happy to slip quietly through. While many people remember images of Tony Abbott in a group hug when the carbon tax was repealed, and of Penny Wong in tears when she was allowed by her party to vote for same-sex marriage, few remember the passage of the Fuel Tax Credit Scheme in 2006 to provide billions of dollars of fossil fuel subsidies. Likewise, were it not for the image of Greens Senator Sarah Hanson-Young holding up a dead salmon, few would remember the passage, with bipartisan support, of Labor's watering down of environmental protection laws in the week before the 2025 election was called, which was also the week of the budget and the opposition's budget-in-reply speech. It's almost as if the major parties hoped the media would be too busy watching the fights about nuclear energy and working from home to spot their agreement on the need to weaken John Howard's environmental laws in order to help the salmon industry continue to pollute the only remaining habitat of the critically endangered Maugean skate.

In the last parliament Labor loved having a big fight with the Greens about its Housing Australia Future Fund (HAFF). Indeed, if Labor's post-election analysis of why the Greens lost three of their lower house seats is believable, then Labor knew that the longer the Greens opposed the passage of the HAFF legislation, the more Greens voters would shift towards Labor. Maybe Labor is right, or maybe the

Greens lost votes in some seats for other reasons, but the key point is that no professional politician would deny there are benefits to having drawn-out fights about issues you think your voters care about. A big fight with your political opponents is one of the few ways that a government can get attention from voters.

Paul Keating once said that politics is the conflict business. And it is precisely because most humans try to avoid conflict that most people struggle to understand that professional politicians, even those declaring their desire to inhabit the sensible centre, love a good stoush. Just as a boxer who won't throw a punch and can't take one won't last long in the ring, the same is true for a politician whose first instinct is to seek compromise the minute someone else makes an ambitious claim.

There is no doubt that Anthony Albanese won over a lot of voters in 2025 — although not nearly as many as Peter Dutton lost — by appearing less combative, more calm and more composed than most of the post-Howard prime ministers. Many in the press gallery underestimated Anthony Albanese, as their predecessors did with John Howard, in part because of his willingness to answer questions at length rather than with cut-through lines that play well on the evening news that few people watch these days.

There is no doubt that Anthony Albanese bested Peter Dutton, but the question in this term of parliament is whether Albo ever really wanted to fight Tories, or whether he is happy to shadow box.

Labor's fourth worst primary vote in 90 years, and its second-best parliamentary majority in 80 years, presents unique opportunities and challenges for the prime minister, his party, and the vast majority of Australians seeking genuine progress rather than endless culture wars.

In a democracy like ours, it is the job of the prime minister to set goals, chart a course and keep things moving. But in the media landscape we are travelling through, it can be hard for voters to keep their bearings, especially when prime ministers, opposition leaders and many of the most powerful industries are happy to keep us stuck in the same old dead ends. Blaming others for an impasse is often a lot easier than looking for a way out, and a great way to maintain the status quo.

It should come as no surprise that the public is largely unaware of how often the parliamentary pantomime of conflict conceals the breadth of bipartisan agreement on big issues like AUKUS, fossil fuel expansion, fossil fuel subsidies, ignoring the fact that unemployment benefits are below the poverty line, failure to fund adequate services for domestic violence, the lack of a wealth tax, and of course the lack of commitment to try other options after the failed Voice referendum. But watch the sparks fly over the $2 billion per year changes to the $60 billion we spend each year on tax concessions for superannuation. Big fights about small things are the safest way to do politics. Yes, they are a step in the right direction, but fights about small things can be a dangerous distraction from the urgent challenges we face.

It's hard for most voters to keep their bearings in a landscape so full of distractions, dead ends and phoney debates. While it's virtually impossible to navigate this terrain with reference to claims of left, right or centre, a safe way to measure progress is to fix your eyes on whether the government is giving the Liberals a veto over its legislation or is willing to work with any senators who are serious about legislating change. Voters need to regularly ask themselves whether the government is letting the perfect be the enemy of the good. Likewise, why would a government determined to drive big change ever claim that their draft bill is so perfect that mere mention of amendments sends them into a tizz?

Julia Gillard achieved far more in her three years in office than most. Her willingness to listen, negotiate, share credit and compromise meant that her government passed far more legislation than the first-term Albanese Government or the Coalition under Morrison. Indeed, the Gillard Government passed some of the most significant legislation in the past half century: creating the NDIS; plain packaging for tobacco; and the Minerals Resource Rent Tax. She also created the Royal Commission into Institutional Responses to Child Sexual Abuse.

While it is rare these days for commentators to talk about Julia Gillard's achievements, preferring to herald the Hawke-Keating years of privatisation and deregulation, when people do discuss the fact that her minority government drove major reforms it is more common to hear suggestions that it was surprising she achieved so much in a minority government rather than a beneficiary of the negotiating possibilities of a power sharing parliament. After the 2010 election, the Gillard Government needed three crossbenchers in the lower house and at least seven votes in the Senate to pass a bill that the Coalition opposed. And unsurprisingly, having negotiated Greens support for legislation in the lower house, not once did the Greens subsequently vote against that bill when it reached the Senate. This meant the legislation always sailed through. Negotiations simply happened earlier, and in turn it was easier to avoid impasse.

Rather than shout "mandate" at the Senate — and complain that she couldn't pass the legislation in the exact form her party room had agreed to — Gillard instead met regularly with the Greens and other crossbenchers to discuss their concerns and their priorities, in the same way she met regularly with her own backbenchers. The result was a parliament that got things done. In admitting she needed to share power Julia Gillard was far more productive in using it.

While the idea that a prime minister might meet with an independent to discuss their concerns is anathema to many, the reality of major party politics is that the final version of the legislation tabled is often radically different from the version first proposed by the department, or even the minister. Backbench Labor, Liberal and National Party MPs often have tantrums, demand amendments, and extract unrelated promises before they agree to support the version of legislation that the public gets to see. But unlike the demands of minor party and independent MPs, the backbench arm-twisting and back scratching is mostly kept out of view. Who can forget the National Party crowing that they had secured $20 billion worth of boondoggles in exchange for Scott Morrison's half-hearted commitment to net zero? Was that evidence-based policy? Centrist? Or just the everyday chaos of majority government that became briefly visible?

Julia Gillard's term is often overlooked by those who prefer men with big mandates driving change to women who can negotiate. History will remember Julia Gillard not just as Australia's first female prime minister, but one of the greatest Labor reformers. What this term in parliament will help shape is how history remembers Anthony Albanese.

After slimming down Bill Shorten's ambitious 2019 agenda to defeat Scott Morrison in 2022, and having smashed Peter Dutton with an even smaller platform of policy reform in 2025, the risk Albanese now faces is if the Senate passes his election promises without any fuss. If the Senate doesn't make a big noise about his small policy proposals, the it's unlikely the public will take much notice of them.

Take housing for example. The seemingly centrist proposal of building 100,000 homes for first-home buyers is easy for the Senate to pass. But will it mean the average childcare worker will ever be able to afford to buy a house in Sydney anywhere near the kids they are paid to care for?

That doesn't mean Labor's housing promises aren't a step in the right direction. And to be clear, it is probably better to do a small thing than to do nothing at all. But the point of governing is to solve problems, not to say things could be worse if you did nothing, and it's hard to believe anyone in Labor actually believes that having built 100,000 homes the intergenerational wealth crisis caused by the current tax treatment of investment properties will vanish. People join the fire brigade to put out fires, not to make the fires a bit smaller than they might have been. Australia needs its political class to be brave enough to take on the challenge of solving big problems, not just telling us things could be worse if someone else was in charge.

Centrist platitudes about babies and bathwater have become the centrepiece of Australian policy debates. They are an insult not just to those citizens who clearly need far more than what has been promised but to those who want to participate in genuine debate about the structural reforms Australia needs to make. If we are serious about making rapid progress on pressing problems, then we need leaders who are brave enough to do bold things, not just good economic managers whose main job is to *manage* our expectations.

More voters clearly believe that Labor's platform and personnel are better for Australia than any other party, but with a primary vote of just 34.6 per cent, it is also clear that nearly two-thirds of Australians wanted something different. Labor's challenge and opportunity in the next three years is to show all Australians that they are willing and able to tackle the big problems we face, not just tinker at the edges.

The collapse in public support for the Coalition in the 2025 election, combined with their record low seat count and the depths of their internal conflicts, mean that the only thing that can make the Coalition relevant in this term of parliament is if the Labor Party insists on obtaining bipartisan support for legislation rather than seeking the simple Senate majority required by the Constitution.

The near irrelevance of the Coalition in federal parliament also creates a significant risk for Labor. To date, Albanese's goal of protecting voters from Scott Morrison in 2022 and Peter Dutton in 2025 was clearly popular enough among swinging voters to win those elections. And in keeping those men from office there is no doubt Labor delivered significantly for most progressive voters who feared the Liberals might further undermine public services, workers' conditions, and Australia's independent place in a rapidly changing world.

Having vanquished the Tories for the first time in decades, Labor, Green and independent voters can dare to dream for significant material improvements to their lives. But if in this term Labor acts as if it is more scared of the fossil fuel industry and the gambling industry than it is of losing progressive voters to the Greens or independents, then the 2028 election is likely to provide another clear example of a wrecking ball knocking down seats in all directions rather than a pendulum that gently shifts marginal seats back and forth between Labor and the Liberals.

The key question for Labor is: do they think they have an enormous mandate to govern, or do they think they only have a small mandate for change?

So, what might an ambitious Labor agenda look like?

The most obvious place to look for good policy that captures Labor's values are policies Labor themselves have previously proposed. Indeed, there is a long list of good policy ideas that Anthony Albanese and most of his cabinet have previously supported, for example:

- Reducing the capital gains tax discount (proposed by Labor in 2016)
- Limiting negative gearing (proposed by Labor in 2016 and a generation earlier in 1985)
- Removing all fossil fuel subsides (Labor signed Australia up to this promise to the G20 in 2009)
- Introducing a $1 limit on poker machine bets (Labor struck an agreement for

this proposal with independent MP Andrew Wilkie in 2010 on the basis of a Productivity Commission report on poker machine reform).

Likewise, the Labor Party's policy platform contains an extensive agenda. In the words of ALP National Secretary Paul Erickson, "The National Platform reflects the progress delivered by the Albanese Government during Labor's first 15 months in power and sets out our long-term aspirations to change Australia for the better".[37] Labor's policy platform makes clear there is support from Labor to:

- Manage Australian gas using codes of conduct, gas reservation policies and security mechanisms
- Invest heavily in the arts and cultural institutions
- Ensure universal access to healthcare (which most experts would agree includes dental health)
- Use "all of the policy levers available to the Commonwealth" to boost younger Australians' access to home ownership.

The list of good ideas that Labor has supported in the past, and that are still included in their party platform, is far longer than the short list above. Indeed, the full list is likely far longer than can be achieved by Labor in just one term, regardless of the size of their majority in the lower house. But the combination of a long list of ways to improve the lives of Australians, combined with a clear policy and political strategy for sequencing them, has the potential to not just keep Labor in power for three or more terms, but to reshape Australia in a way that we have not seen for decades. As Anthony Albanese said in his foreword to his policy platform:

> We may be Australia's oldest political party but as Labor people we have always mapped our history in achievements, not years. We look with pride on a rich legacy of reforms that have improved the lives of Australians to such a profound extent they have become part of the national story: Medicare, the NDIS, accessible education, universal superannuation, the *Sex Discrimination Act*, the *Racial Discrimination Act*, Native Title,

> the Apology to the Stolen Generations, and saving the Franklin River …
>
> We look to our history as a party, not out of nostalgia but because it reminds us of what is possible when we have the discipline, courage, vision and ambition for our nation to persuade the Australian people that we are worthy of staying the course.

The Albanese Government has the constitutional right to introduce any legislation it desires, and if it can pass that legislation through the Senate, by one vote or unanimously, that legislation will become the law of the land. Just as Whitlam's *Racial Discrimination Act*, Australia Council for the Arts and Medibank — which became Medicare — and Gillard's NDIS are still in place and still helping millions of Australians, so too can the Albanese Government's legacy shape Australia for decades to come.

Or not.

Instead of working with progressive votes in the Senate to craft a shared agenda there is nothing in the Constitution that says the prime minister should be brave or push for anything at all. Indeed, if he wants to spend three years complaining that the Greens and Liberals won't respect his mandate, he has the constitutional right to do just that. Such a strategy of doing little but complaining much would no doubt attract significant praise from conservative business and media interests whose best hope now that the Liberals have self-destructed is for Labor to self-regulate its ambitions. What could be better for conservatives than a progressive government that seeks permission from the Liberals and Nationals before pursuing major reform?

Australia is one of the richest countries in the world and there is nothing in our Constitution, nothing about our economy, and nothing about the stated desires of Australian voters that stops us from having nice things like free dental care, free childcare and a genuinely low-carbon economy. But as long as our elected representatives interpret centrism to mean bipartisan support, instead of good ideas with strong public support, then the prospects for progressive change are slim.

Time is of the essence.

Australia is not just rich and lucky; it faces unique and daunting challenges in the decades ahead. No matter how much free gas we give away or how much we spend on fossil fuel subsidies, the world will transition away from coal and gas in the coming decades. Whether it is the foreign gas industry or Australian taxpayers who profit from the final years of fossil fuels is up to us. The Saudis think the way to get rich from oil is to restrict supply, drive up the price and collect as much for Saudi Arabia as they can. In Australia we hear that the more gas we export, and the less tax we collect, the more competitive we will be. One country is completely wrong.

Australia has also placed big risky bets on the longevity of US interest in our part of the world. While no one can predict the future, having seen how the US is willing to treat its allies in Canada and Europe, not to mention its humiliation of Ukraine, it is hard to believe that there remains bipartisan support in Australia for a $360 billion contract for nuclear submarines which rely so heavily on the goodwill of the US to deliver, maintain and deploy.

In short, Australia faces big challenges and big opportunities that require more bravery and boldness than the last few decades of centrism have been able to muster. While avoiding conflict, seeking the lowest common denominator, and blaming others for any lack of progress might make governing easy, it will make the choices Australia faces in the future much harder.

The Albanese Government has a unique opportunity to come clean with the Australian public about the breadth of the choices and challenges we face and then chart a course not through the centre, but towards the country the prime minister wants us to be. And if he has to fight a few Tories along the way, it's proof he is heading in the right direction. As former US President Franklin Delano Roosevelt once said, "Judge me by the enemies I have made".[38]

Of course, centrism means never having to pick a side, never making a powerful enemy, never losing big fights. And, inevitably, never winning them. But democracy thrives on high expectations, and if the prime minister picks the right fights and makes the right enemies, then he won't just rebuild our economy and society, he will rebuild Australians' faith in the role of democracy in improving people's lives. Given the world we are now living in, could anything be more important than that?

Endnotes

1 McKnight (2005) *Beyond Right and Left*, p 5

2 "Seizing the Moment" (2023) Canberra Writers Festival panel

3 Peetz (2016) "Industrial action, the right to strike, ballots and the *Fair Work Act* in international context", *Australian Journal of Labour Law*, vol. 29, no. 2:133—53.

4 *The New Daily* (2025) "Liberal leadership could become a three-way race" https://www.thenewdaily.com.au/news/politics/australian-politics/2025/05/12/liberal-leadership-could-become-a-three-way-race

5 Jaspan (2025) "Who's backing who? Every major newspaper's pick for prime minister", *Sydney Morning Herald*, https://www.smh.com.au/business/companies/who-s-backing-who-every-newspaper-s-pick-for-prime-minister-20250501-p5lvup.html

6 Staszewska (2024) "What we know about Australia's only live nuclear reactor", https://www.sbs.com.au/news/article/what-we-know-about-australias-only-live-nuclear-reactor/valo6klpo

7 Sky News Australia (2025) "The Coalition is 'wisely asserting' the need for nuclear power", https://www.

youtube.com/watch?v=LrbgOqaYQwo

8 Hern (2020) "Berlin artist uses 99 phones to trick Google into traffic jam alert", https://www.theguardian.com/technology/2020/feb/03/berlin-artist-uses-99-phones-trick-google-maps-traffic-jam-alert

9 Hartcher (2022) "Radioactive", https://www.smh.com.au/politics/federal/radioactive-inside-the-top-secret-aukus-subs-deal-20220510-p5ak7g.html

10 Sinha (2016) *The Slave's Cause: A History of Abolition*, p 3

11 Guterres (2018) Secretary-General's remarks on Climate Change, https://www.un.org/sg/en/content/sg/statement/2018-09-10/secretary-generals-remarks-climate-change-delivered

12 Guterres (2023) UN Press Conference on Climate, https://news.un.org/en/story/2023/06/1137747

13 Australia Institute "Australia's gas policy mess | Fact sheet", 21 October 2024, https://australiainstitute.org.au/post/australias-gas-policy-mess-fact-sheet/; Sier (2025) "'Major shift in our understanding': Japan resells more Australian gas", https://www.afr.com/world/asia/japan-ramps-up-regional-reselling-of-australian-gas-20250519-p5m0d4

14 Di Stefano (2023) "News Corp tabloids struggle to hit ambitious subscriptions targets", https://www.afr.com/companies/media-and-marketing/news-corp-tabloids-struggle-to-hit-ambitious-subscriptions-targets-20230816-p5dx1x

15 *Sydney Morning Herald* (2009) "Garrett gives nod to uranium mine", https://www.smh.com.au/national/garrett-gives-nod-to-uranium-mine-20090715-dk9y.html

16 Mitchell (2015) "Peter Garrett uses TV interview",

https://www.smh.com.au/politics/federal/peter-garrett-says-kevin-rudd-was-a-danger-to-australia-in-tv-interview-20151011-gk6i04.html

17 *Sydney Morning Herald* (2010) "Wong backs Labor's anti-gay marriage stance", https://www.smh.com.au/politics/federal/wong-backs-labors-antigay-marriage-stance-20100725-10q37.html

18 Penny Wong quoted in James Massola (2024) "Wong on Payman: She should vote with us, like I had to on gay marriage", https://www.smh.com.au/politics/federal/wong-reminds-payman-she-opposed-same-sex-marriage-before-labor-supported-it-20240627-p5jpaj.html

19 Pearse (2007) "What turned the Liberal Party off climate change action?", https://www.crikey.com.au/2007/11/16/what-turned-the-liberal-party-off-climate-change-action/

20 Tiffen (2011) "Four climate change positions in one day", https://www.smh.com.au/politics/federal/four-climate-change-positions-in-one-day-20110309-1bnu3.html

21 Crowe (2024) "Albanese unlikely to announce new climate targets until after federal election", https://www.smh.com.au/politics/federal/albanese-unlikely-to-announce-new-climate-targets-until-after-federal-election-20241116-p5kr4t.html

22 Chan (2015) "Labor conference rejected push for federal anti-corruption commission", https://www.theguardian.com/australia-news/2015/jul/29/labor-conference-rejected-push-federal-anti-corruption-commission

23 Gary Gray quoted in Deborah Snow and James Robertson (2015) "'Choppergate' puts politicians'

perks under scrutiny", https://www.smh.com.au/politics/federal/choppergate-puts-politicians-perks-under-scrutiny-20150724-gijj5o.html

24 Australia Institute (2016) "Polling: Voters support a national ICAC", https://australiainstitute.org.au/report/polling-voters-support-a-national-icac/

25 *The Saturday Paper* (2018) "Shorten pledges anti-corruption body"; Turnbull (2018) Doorstop interview at Thomas Global Systems, https://pmtranscripts.pmc.gov.au/release/transcript-41431

26 Karp (2021) "Coalition accused of breaking promise", https://www.theguardian.com/australia-news/2021/nov/20/coalition-accused-of-breaking-promise-on-federal-integrity-commission

27 McLeod (2022) "Integrity watchdog will only hold public hearings in 'exceptional' circumstances", https://www.news.com.au/national/politics/integrity-watchdog-will-only-hold-public-hearings-in-exceptional-circumstances/news-story/bb6e7e3c5089699dce53f5c301d3f81d

28 Griffiths and Chan (2023) "Big money was spent on the 2022 election — but the party with the deepest pockets didn't win", https://theconversation.com/big-money-was-spent-on-the-2022-election-but-the-party-with-the-deepest-pockets-didnt-win-198780

29 Keane (2025) "The last of Palmer: A quarter-billion dollars of political dilettantism", https://www.crikey.com.au/2025/05/07/clive-palmer-trumpet-of-patriots-united-australia-party-donald-trump/

30 Karp (2024) "After a year of fighting, the Greens grant most of PM's Christmas wishes in late bill flurry", https://www.theguardian.com/

australia-news/2024/nov/29/after-a-year-of-fighting-the-greens-grant-most-of-pms-christmas-wishes-in-late-bill-flurry

31 Roy and Jennett (2025) "Katy Gallagher seeks fourth Senate win at federal election, but concedes Pocock's popularity", https://www.abc.net.au/news/2025-04-25/labor-senator-katy-gallagher-federal-election-pitch/105213136

32 Australia Institute (2025) "Polling — Truth in political advertising", https://australiainstitute.org.au/report/polling-truth-in-political-advertising-2/

33 Australia Institute (2021) "Polling — ACT Senate Representation", https://australiainstitute.org.au/wp-content/uploads/2022/10/Australia-Institute-4August2021-ACT.pdf

34 Department of Employment and Workplace Relations (2022) "Major workplace relations reform bill is now an Act", https://www.dewr.gov.au/newsroom/articles/major-workplace-relations-reform-bill-now-act

35 Department of Employment and Workplace Relations (2024) "Fact sheet: Right to disconnect", https://www.dewr.gov.au/closing-loopholes/resources/right-disconnect

36 Kehoe (2021) "Liberal governments outspend Labor on COVID-19 stimulus", https://www.afr.com/policy/economy/liberal-governments-outspend-labor-on-covid-19-stimulus-20210304-p577pr

37 Australian Labor Party, *ALP National Platform*, 49th National Conference, p 2, https://www.alp.org.au/media/3569/2023-alp-national-platform.pdf

38 Roosevelt (1932) Campaign address on public utilities and development of hydro-electric power,

Portland, https://www.presidency.ucsb.edu/documents/campaign-address-portland-oregon-public-utilities-and-development-hydro-electric-power

Acknowledgements

Research is a team sport and I couldn't have written this essay without the amazing Australia Institute team behind me and, of course, without the thousands of donors who make all our work possible.

In particular I must single out Josh Black who has provided invaluable support as a research assistant and providing thoughtful and detailed responses to early drafts. Thanks also to Bill Browne for sage advice and reflections on contemporary Australian democracy and to Skye Predavec for assistance with number-crunching the results for the 2025 election, especially as they kept changing before our very eyes.

Leeanne Minshull provided insightful feedback on drafts and Amy Remeikis helped me get my head straight, and keep it straight, as I tried to get my head around what centrists are thinking. Finally, this essay would not have been possible without the advice, editing and focus of Alice Grundy who even managed to keep me to deadline.

About the author

Dr Richard Denniss is a prominent Australian economist, Executive Director of The Australia Institute, author and public policy commentator. He has spent the last 20 years moving between policy-focused roles in academia, federal politics and think tanks. He was also a Lecturer in Economics at the University of Newcastle and former Associate Professor in the Crawford School of Public Policy at ANU. He is a regular contributor to *The Monthly* and the author of several books including *Econobabble*, *Curing Affluenza* and *Dead Right: How Neoliberalism Ate Itself and What Comes Next?*

About The Australia Institute

The Australia Institute conducts research that drives the public debate and secures policy outcomes to make Australia better.

The Australia Institute's independence and nonpartisanship ensure our work is guided by a vision for a fairer Australia, without political or commercial influence. Our research regularly calls into question powerful vested interests, multinational corporations, and the economic orthodoxy.

This work is only possible because of independent donations. The support of our donors powers the Institute's ability to fulfill its motto: research that matters. To contribute to our work and ongoing research, you can make a donation on our website by scanning the QR code below.

Vantage Point Issue 1

After America: Australia and the new world order
Emma Shortis
May 2025

Australian political leaders have bent the knee at the altar of American global leadership for decades, placing the ANZUS treaty at the centre of the nation's security. AUKUS has become the latest symbol of strategic solidarity. For Australia's governments, of whatever political persuasion, America continues to define the global rules-based order.

Now that the American people have elected Donald Trump as the forty-seventh president, how will his presidency affect Australia's foreign policy, trade, climate action and approach to human rights? More importantly, will Australia be able to act in its own interests, or will it simply defer to Trump's idea of America?

Dr Emma Shortis draws on her long-standing research on America's place in the world, her discussions with some of Australia's most prominent policy-makers and commentators and her experience in America in the final days of the election campaign, to develop a picture of how the world is changing with a second Trump presidency and what choices Australia has in determining its own future.

Vantage Point Issue 3

Aiming Higher: Universities and the Future of Australian Democracy

George Williams

Decades of policy decisions have made access to higher education harder for those who need it most.

Public trust and community confidence in universities in Australia and overseas are at all-time lows.

Political sentiment has shifted. Our centres of higher learning have leapfrogged big business to become easy political targets. And it's no surprise; the sector has scored its fair share of own goals over the handling of staff underpayment, Vice-Chancellor salaries, antisemitism, free speech and safety on campus.

Ad hoc and insufficient government funding has forced universities down the path of corporatisation, drifting away from their role as public institutions with the mission to serve the public good.

Professor George Williams, drawing on his expertise in Australian constitutional law and democracy, outlines necessary changes to Australian higher education. Universities need to claim agency, tackle the issues within their control, and replace self-interest with a genuine commitment to putting their students and communities first. Without a reset the future looks grim. Our universities need to guard against misinformation and foster the next generation; the nation requires critical thinkers, researchers and innovators more than ever.

Available in November 2025

Australia Institute
Press

Become a subscriber

- Receive four thought-provoking essays from leading experts each year
- Short enough to read in one or two sittings, long enough for in-depth analysis
- Free postage within Australia

Australia Institute Press

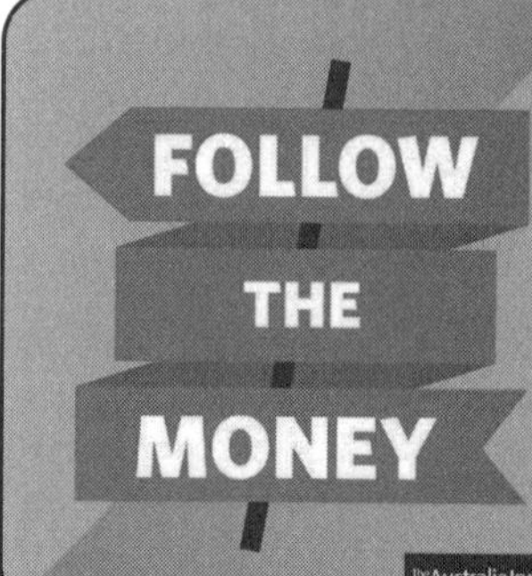

DOLLARS & SENSE

with Greg Jericho

The Australia Institute
Research that matters

Vantage Point: Issue 2

Read it and pass it on. Put your name and email below and start a conversation with other readers.

Name	Contact